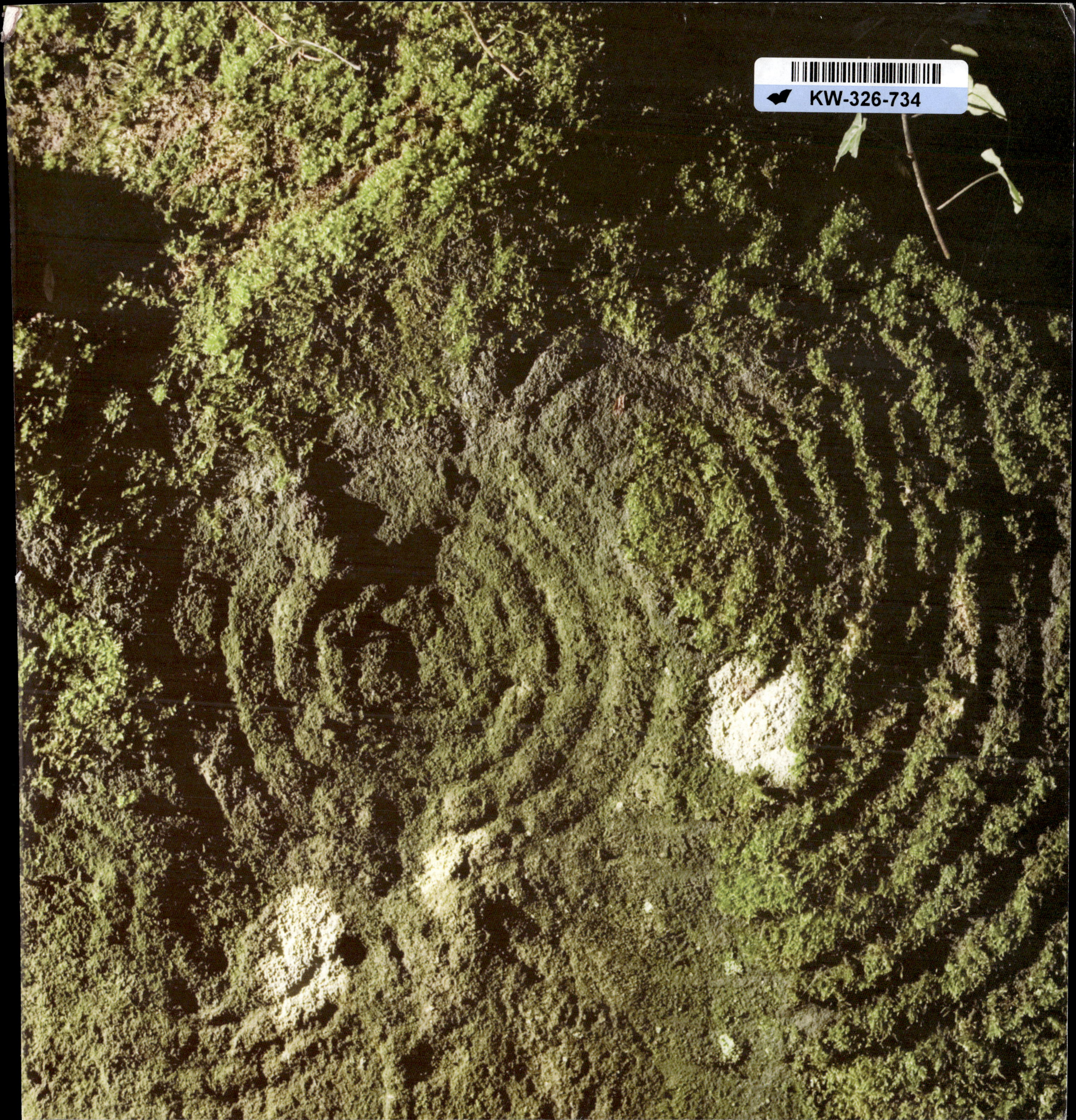

Foreword - Reambra

As chairman of the Tyrone GAA County Board Committee, it gives me great pleasure to write a few words by way of welcoming this excellent pictorial and poetic publication to commemorate the visit of the Sam Maguire cup to the historic county of Tyrone.

I congradulate the authors Frank Quinn and Kathleen Burns on completion of a truly unique piece of work which brought them to every corner of County Tyrone to bring to life our National Heritage and uncover some of Tyrone's hidden jewels .

Readers, young and old will truly enjoy this journey. Compilation of such a comprehensive gallery of photographs and anecdotal material involved a significant amount of time and travel by the authors.

Frank and Kathleen are to be commended for their professionalism and research in bringing to life our heritage for the benefit of current and future generations.

This book will also be of immense benefit to tourists visiting Tyrone.

Guim gach rath agus blath oraibh
Padraig Ó Dorchai,
Cathaoirleach, Coiste Thir Eoghain

Introduction

In picture, verse, song and prayer, we are proud to tell a story about the county of Tyrone in a way never told before.

We set out to photograph the Sam Maguire Cup in a variety of settings in the beautiful landscape of Tyrone, particularly in the Sperrin Mountains, one of the richest areas in Ireland for prehistoric monuments and archaeological remains. Our aim was to capture something of the history and ancient spirit of Tyrone by picturing the Cup against the background of some of our most famous prehistoric monuments, and in the context of other more recent remains such as Old Castles, Ancestral Homes, Church and Monastic Ruins, Old Abbeys, High Crosses, Graveyards and Ancient Forts, Mass Rocks, Mass Gardens and Holy Wells. The rich heritage of Tyrone is evidenced not only in an abundance of material remains but also in a diverse legacy of musical styles and dance forms with Irish and Scottish roots, a profound literary tradition and a wealth of folklore and tradition. Literature and writing has a long history in the Sperrins: at Aughnascribba ("Field of the Writing"), for example, a form of ancient writing (Ogham) can be found etched in stone.

A century ago, thousands of native speakers of Irish inhabited the remote glens and mountain fastnesses of the Sperrins and interest in the language remains strong today. The expanding Gaelscoil movement bears witness to the commitment of Tyrone people to the old tongue as a new generation of young Irish speakers begin to emerge from the educational system.

Some of the engravings that can be seen on the Sam Maguire Cup are reminiscent of the style of decorative designs featuring in the Book of Kells, dating back more than 1,200 years. The linking of this famous Book and famous Cup in this way renders it doubly fitting to place "Sam" in the historical settings we have chosen for him here.

People today have a strong interest in and feeling for the sites and stones of our ancient past. These Megalithic Tombs, Stone Circles and Standing Stones are often shrouded in mystery and, by the same token, the lives of the people who erected them are hidden from us for the most part – all the more to excite the imagination and inspire a sense of wonder and admiration as we view these remainders of an ancient culture in our own day, in our own place.

It is our hope that this book will not only serve to stimulate increased interest in and concern for the ancient places of Tyrone and its Irish culture, but also capture something of the beauty of the County in its many moods.

Contents

Aughascribba Ogham Standing Stone: (1000BC-500AD)

Greencastle - (Caislean)

Aughnascribba - Field of Writing

Ogham was a form of writing which spans the pre-historic to early christian period.

Ancient guardians
of time and secrets,
the stone giants
lean and whisper
of their youth

Looking back across the years on our stones
People still have deep feelings for these ancient stones
even though they do not understand their mysteries.

Beaghmore Stone Circles (dating back to 1500BC)

Beaghmore - (Beitheach mor) - Large birch land

Beaghmore, Dunamore, Cookstown

These stone circles are a reflection of the ritual and spiritual life in the early Bronze age.

The alignments of these stone circles are unknown but they apparently align with the rising sun on or about the 30th of May.

'The Beaghmore Stone Circle'

Around by Beagh Rock in the Country Tyrone
Are numbers of circles and big standing stones
At Micheal McMahon's they stand by the score
About his wee farm around by Beaghmore.

The stones were set up before any peat grew.
And just have a look and you'll find it is true
The most of them's neatly set up on their end
And some people say by the bold beaker men.

by Geordie Barnett

Collected by Peter Smith and Francis Clarke from the late Joe O Neill (Joe Phat Ghearrfheidh - Broughdearg)

Clogherny Wedge Tomb (2000BC), Plumbridge

Clogherny - (Cloch airne) - A stony place where sloes grow

Close to the Buttlerlope Glen

Butterlope Glen

'*The Mountain*'

To the mountain I've seen summer coming,
The glories of nature in bloom;
The bees through the heather bells humming;
The scent of the bracken and broom.
And, oh, but I'm proud of my sireland-
Its beauties I claim as my own;
And first to my heart in all Ireland
The mountains of Co Tyrone.

by Felix Kearney

Loughash Wedge Tomb, Donemana

Donemana - (Dunamanagh) - The fort of the monks

Turn and look back, You'll see horizons
Much like the ones they saw,
The tomb - builders, millenniums ago
The channel scratched by rain, the same old
Sediment of dusk, winter returning.

Silverbrook Mills, Donemana

Donemana - (Dunamanagh) - The fort of the monks

"An industrial past - All is Quiet now"

The Mill

T'was the County Tyrone I was born in,
A County unequalled for fun.
It was there on a bright harvest morning
My earthly adventures begun.

Away back in the dark misty ages
The mill it was always the same
Aye and judging from history's pages
A place of great learning and fame.

by Felix Kearney.

The village of Sion Mills came into existence in 1835, when the Flax Spinning Mill was built
here astride the River Mourne, which has helped to turn the wheels, and has brought prosperity to the place for a century and a quarter.

Glenroan Portal Tomb, Plumbridge (3000 - 2500 BC)

Glenroan - (Glean Ruadhan) - Red Glen

Often referred to as "Gleann Sroine" Glen of the nose,
because it is the only projection for many miles along the valley

Along the lane, beneath the trees
Beside the busy, noisy road,
Untouched, untroubled, unaware;
New life appearing all around
And though grey clouds may fill the
sky or creeping mist obscure the hills.

Plumbridge : where did it come from?
The story goes that a man named Devine built the bridge without the benefit of a Spirit Level.

Ballinderry River

Ballinderry River - A famous salmon and trout resort

It rises in the foothills of the Sperrin mountains and twists its way through rocky Kildress down to the soils around the Lough Neagh basin, where it empties itself.

Rivers flow all through the night
Never weary or tired they be.
Rivers can meander away
Curling twisting night and day
On their journey to meet the sea.

This bridge links County Tyrone and County Derry

Clady Bridge

This bridge links County Tyrone and County Donegal

Lackagh Old Church & Stone Carvings

Drumquin - Droim Caoin - Pleasant Ridge

"Early Seventeeth Century Church"

We are not always ready
For the things that God has planned;
They are sometimes unexpected
And we do not understand.

But always there's a purpose
Which as yet we may not see;
It's locked away from vision,
But God's love provides the key.

The church probably dates to the early seventeenth century but has more likely been constructed on the sight of the earlier Christian Period and medieval churches. There is a stone carving in the graveyard to the southeast of the church building. On one face, the carving depicts two figures in profile; on the other they appear to be wrestling. They may represent Jacob wrestling with the angel, a scene that appears on a number of the high crosses. According to local tradition, the stone is supposed to mark the grave of Siamese twins. It may date to the Early Christian Period.

The smell of burning heather in the spring

Comes the glory of the summer, bringing beauty in its train,
The beauty that a child can love and know.
The hedgerows are a - shimmer as the flowers bloom again
And your heart is filled with dreams of long ago.

by Felix Kearney

Peatlands Park Centre gives an insight into the fascinating development of bogs and peat land.
Island Turf Craft Bog Musuem in Coalisland-Marvel at the treasure trove of artefacts related to the rich history of Ireland before and after the Ice Age.

Peatlands Park, Dungannon
Take to the bogs! See the wonders of nature

The Brantry Lough

The Brantry Lough, it has beauty spots
And they are a sight to see.
But undoubtedly the Brantry Lough
Is the one most dear to me.

This lough is not the only one
That you should come to see,
For there are many other sights
In the dear old Brantry.

Dungannon Gates, Dungannon

Dungannon - (Dun geanainn) - Geannan's fort

Pat Mulgrew Pictured

The Cottage on the auld Dungannon Road.

I'm sitting in my English home, surrounded by dear friends,
With all that wealth and title God can bring,
But I seem to be ungrateful to God who's goodness sends.
Me, my many gifts and exiles hearts to cheer.
My heart is far from here, I can never feel at rest,
I n'er could call this country my abode,
For my heart keeps going westward with every passing breeze
To that Cottage on the auld Dungannon Road.

For I'm tired of city life with all its sweat and sin
Fain would I lay down my heavy load
To live in peace and comfort, the remainder of my life
In the Cottage on the auld Dungannon Road.

Dr Seamus Mac Mathuna, Dungannon is director of Celtic Studies in the University of Ulster, Coleraine was co editor along with Ailbhe O Corrain of the Collins Pocket Irish Dictionary (1995). | Other people from Dungannon are Birdy Sweeney - Actor, Darren Clarke - Professional Golfer, Ryan Farquhar - Motorbike Racer, Victor Sloan - Artist, Adrian Logan and Joanne Salley - TV Presenters. Austin Currie, Edendork, is the only Irish politician who served in both political administrations north and south of the border. | Charlie Donnelly, a poet from the Edendork area, was killed at the battle of the Jarama Front, during the Spanish Civil War 1937. He had been part of an Irish delegation assisting the socialist movement in the war. | Art McCrory a former Tyrone County GAA manager hails from Dungannon. | Iggy Jones a renowned GAA player was also from Dungannon.

Peadar Joe Haughey's Cottage

Creggan - (An Creagan) - Little crag

"The last native gaelic speaker in the Parish"

When I stammered my school Irish
One Sunday after mass, crinkled
A rusty litany of praise:
Ta an Ghaeilge againn aris…

by J Montague

Johnny Ban Mc Aleer of Moin na Miol near Glenhull spoke the native dialect of County Tyrone.
According to the Census 1821, the total inhabitants in Tyrone was 261,865 of which it was estimated that about 140,000 were Irish speakers.

Dun Uladh Cultural Heritage Centre, Killyclogher

Dun Uladh Culture heritage centre is where the visitor learns about music, literature and other cultural aspects of the area. It contains a small museum, gallery and library.

The Ceilidh House

There is a wee house by the road side
Where I ceilidhed within
White walls and white gables
And thatched to the brim

The house it would fill
And the craic it would begin
As more of the neighbours
Would let themselves in.

by P Montague

Various events take place through the summer months, held nearby at Teach Ceoil in Rouskey, expressing cultural identity through song and story.

St. Dympna's Church, Dromore

Dromore - (Droim mor) - The great ridge

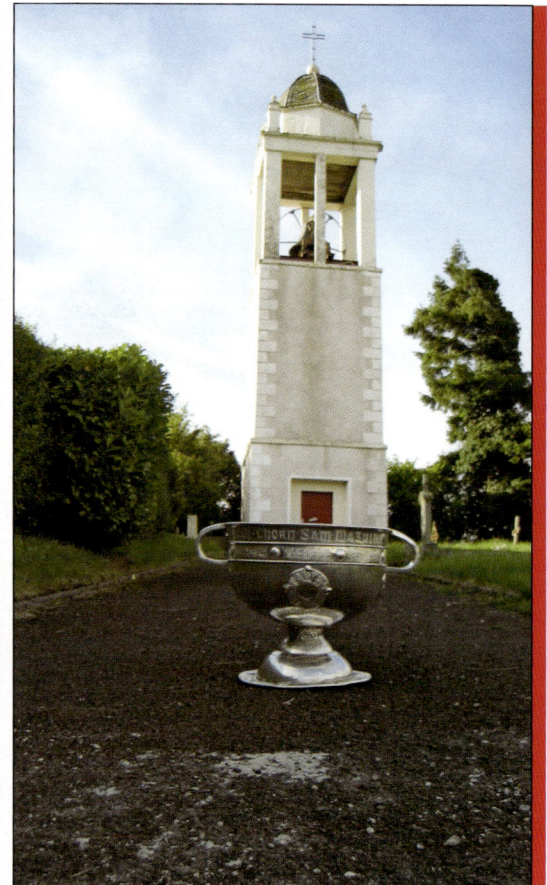

Enduring

Pious builders of our Churches
Raised their towers and steeples high
So that we should be reminded,
When we look towards the sky,
That they stand, eternal symbols,
While we mortals live and die.

Seamus Donaghy legendry gaelic footballer was born in Dromore.

34

Donaghmore High Cross
A Composite Cross - Donaghmore

Donaghmore - (Domhnach Mor) - Big Church

The Celtic cross carved with Biblical Scenes was an early visual aid in Christian Teaching

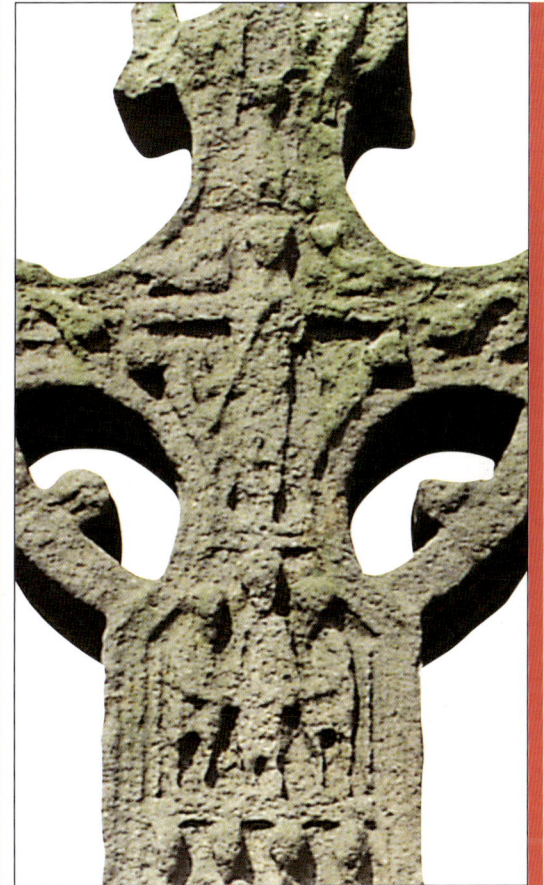

A church stands near,
By the road, an ancient cross.

by William Butler Yeats

An t-Athair Eamonn O Doibhlin author of the comprehensive study of Domhnach Mor wrote extensively in Irish for An t-Ultach and other publications. It was a house in Drumbearn, near Domhnach Mor where the Franscian Friars lived in the 18th Century.

Ballywholan Chambered Grave, Clogher

Clogher - (Clochar) - Stone place

They bide their time in
Green lanes and fields.
Pitted stones, grey, ochre-patched
With moss, lodged for lose spirits.

Ancient Monuments
Straddling Centuries

Ruins of Trillick Castle

Built around 1630. Now only some ruins exist of Trillick Castle

The ruined castle

Oh! let me sigh to think this ruin'd pile
Was favour'd once with fortune's radiant smile;
These moss-grown battlements, these ivy'd towers,
Have seen prosperity's uncertain hours.

Trillick - (Trileac) - Three Stones
At the foot of Brougher Mountain

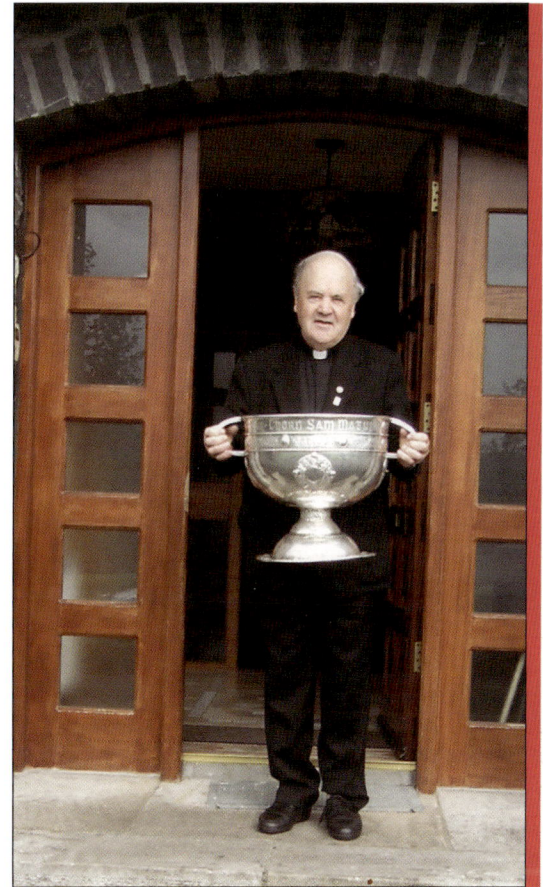

The Priest's Leap

The priest is out upon the hill before the dawn of day;
Through shadows deep, o'er rugged ground, he treads his painful way;
A peasant's homely garb he wears, that none but friendly eyes
May know who dares to walk abroad beneath that rough disguise;
Inside his coat and near his heart lies what he treasures most,
For there a tiny silver case enshrines the Sacred Host.

In Trillick - Some of the oldest gravestones mark out the final resting place of members of the O Neill Clan.
Kilskeery cemetery - A site of historical interest.
Father John McKenna - Pictured

Ruins of a Tower House at Castlehill, Dungannon

Dungannon - (Dun Geanainn) - Geannan's fort

The 10th Century. Chief seat of the O Neill's of Tyrone.

Tir Eoghain: Land of Owen,
Province of the O'Niall;
The ghostly tread of O'Hagan's
Barefoot gallowglasses marching
To merge forces in Dun Geanainn.

by John Montague

Spring Well - Pictured below

Castle built in 1305 and abandoned by Hugh O Neill in 1607, shortly before the Flight of the Earls. | Crosscavanagh -Home of the O' Neill's from the eleventh century, before they moved to Dungannon.. | All O'Neill's castles had their own spring well. | At one stage Dungannon was said to be the centre of power in Ireland because of the O'Neill dynasty.

St. Patrick's Chair and Well

Favor Royal Forest, Augher

Auger - (Eachradh)

"A Throne like Rock"

May the Irish hills caress you.
may her lakes and rivers bless you.
may the luck of the Irish enfold you.
may the blessings of Saint Patrick behold you.

"Holy wells are sacred places that deserve honour and care"

Eugene McKenna former Tyrone Captain, All Ireland finalist and former Tyrone manager is from Augher.
James McKenna - Pictured

41

Old Church Bell, Beragh
Beragh - (Bearach) - The place of Birch trees

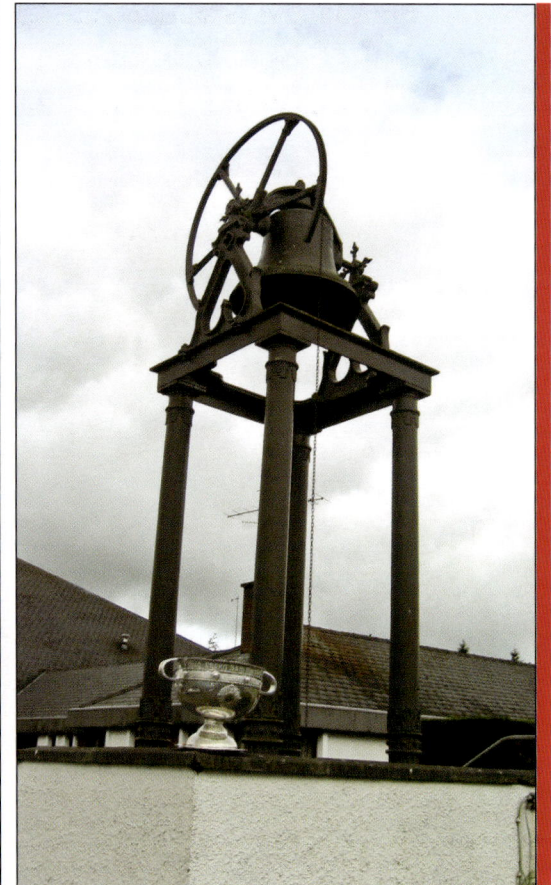

As the iron bell
Swings out again, each quarter's note
Dwindling down a shaft of past
And present, to drown
In that throat of stone.

by John Montague

Des Mc Mahon, the chief design architect for Croke Park, Dublin is from Beragh

Sixmilecross

Sixmilecross - (Na Corracha Mora) - The big round hills

Sixmilcross is said to have got its name from a celtic cross which stood in a field at the top of the village 6 Irish miles from Omagh, hence, "Six Mile Cross".

Jackie Heaney - Famous Tyrone referee

*The sun's red rim
Is hidden soon,
The low clouds dim
The rising moon.
Shy badgers hide
Still in their den,
But rabbits glide
Through Bernish Glen.*

by W F Marshall

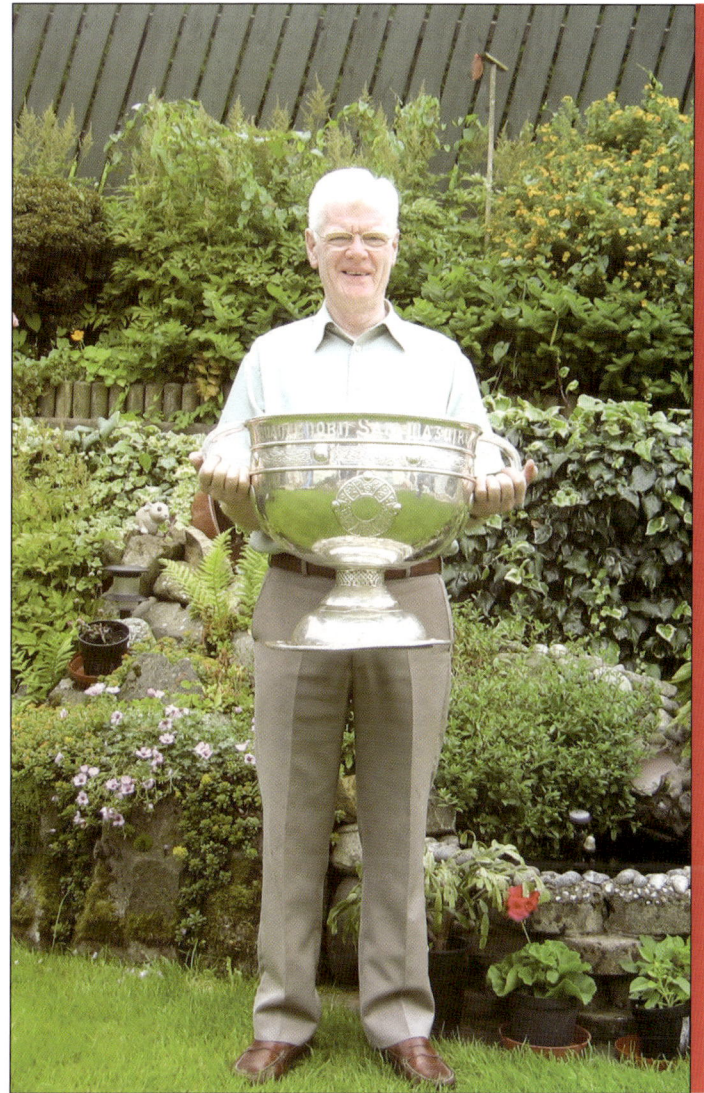

A famous local poet and minister, William Forbes Marshall, whose birthplace is the old school house in the town, penned many famous poems while living in the area, and today, visitors can travel along "The Marshall Country Trail" stopping at the many features which provided inspiration for his works.

Coyles Cottage, Ardboe

Ardboe - (Achadh bho) - Field of the cows

"A 300 years old fisherman's cottage" situated on the shores of Lough Neagh. Built primarily of mud walls, supported by four corners built of stone which were whitewashed to help withstand the weathering. The thatch is a local Lough shore reed which was used because of its durability.

Just Think

Can you imagine how dull it would be
To dwell in a country without any sea.
How lucky we are to have the shores that extend,
From Old Ardboe to beautiful Toomebridge
And boats full of eels for all to share.

Níl aon tin teán mar do thin teán féin

Gortin Lakes, Gortin

Gortin - (An Goirtin) - Little tilled field

Drop a pebble in water; just a splash, and it is gone,
But there's half-a-hundred ripples circling on and on and on,
Kindness spreading from the centre, flowing on and out to the sea,
And there's no sure way of telling where the end is going to be.

The Gortin Lakes are a cluster of Kattlehole Lakes left by uneven melting of retreating ice.

Gortin Glen Forest, Gortin

Gortin - (An Goirtin) - Little tilled field

"Gortin is one of the most picturesque villages in County Tyrone, sited on the banks of the Owenkillew River".

There's Gortin Glens, with its romantic scenes
Down its shaggy rocks bright streams are flowin'
With Seskinore and sweet Dromore
Ant the mossy hills in fair Tyrone.

by Jimmy Jinny Devlin
Fallagh Gortin

The Servite Priory, Benburb

Benburb - (Beannbhorb) - Bold peak.

This beautiful old manor house was purchased in 1947 by Fr. James Keane, on behalf of the Servite Order to open a foundation in Ireland. The Priory was opened in 1949. Since coming to Benburb the servites have maintained an "open door" policy to all of the community regardless of class, politics religion and the Priory is seen as a haven where people can come and feel welcome.

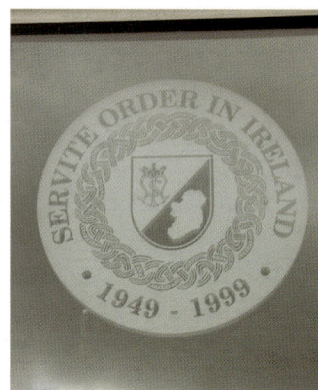

God take your hands in trouble,
In turmoil and in strife,
And may the comfort of his love
Forever fill your life.

The Servites of Benburb are dedicated to promoting healing and reconciliation.
Fr Colm McDonnell and Fr Chris O'Brien - Pictured

The famous 'Salmon Leap' on the River Blackwater

My place of clear water...
by Seamus Heaney

Moy

Moy - (Mao) - Plain

Motorists passing through the village of Moy, ought to stop at the bottom of the hill and admire the cast-iron gate set up in the 19th century to provide the grand entrance to the now-vanished Roxborough Castle.

The great mart for the purchase of good horses was in the fair of Moy.
Eileen Donaghy the famed country singer and the mother of the great footballer Plunkett Donaghy is from the Moy.

Fishing in the Blackwater River

Knockmany Passage Tomb, (Annia' Cove), Clogher

Knockmany - (Cnoc manaigh) - The monk's hill

Where a community about whom we know very little carved mysterious messages on massive rocks, then stood them around their burial and closed it over.

Queen Baine of Clogher is said to be buried in a chambered cairn in Knockmany Forest.

Over all this valley, stands Knockmany Hill.
It's crown is a chambered tomb.

Knockmany, my darling I see you again,
As the sunrise has made you a King;
And your proud face looks tenderly down on the plain
Where my young larks are learning to sing.

By Rose Kavanagh

Benburb Castle, Benburb

Benburb - (Beann burb) - Proud or bold cliff

The Northern Blackwater

Oh! the broom banks of the river are fair,
Now the wild briar is blossoming there -
Now when the green banks so calmly repose,
Lulled by the rivers strange chant as it goes.

by Rose Kavanagh

The Castle now stands in ruined beauty on the grounds of the Servite Priory Benburb.
It was an O'Neill site on the northern bank of the River Blackwater.

Tyrone Crystal, Killybrackey, Dungannon

The Craft of Crystal

Engraved or cut in newest taste,
Or plain —whichever pleases best;
Lustres repaired or polished bright,
And broken glasses matched at sight;
Hall globes of every size and shape.
by Marsden Haddock

Trade circular in verse 1790

Roughan Castle

Overlooking Roughan Lough

Newmills

Roughan Castle

Here stands a ruined castle in stately Roughan Park
The princely home of Phelim O'Neill when Irish skies were dark,
No more an alien hand shall till that lovely verdant sod
Or tend the flocks round Roughan Park where Phelim reigned as lord.

The version above is that of the late Maggie Shields of Brockagh.

Newmills takes its name from a corn mill and kilns which formerly stood in the area.

Castlederg Castle, Castlederg

Castlederg - (Caislean na Deirge) - Castle of the river

A site previously occupied by an O' Neill tower house.

Close by is the White Standing Stone, Kilcroagh and Leitrim Portal Tomb (The Druid's Altar).

Dunamore Wedge Tomb
(Dermot and Grainne's bed), Cookstown
Dunamore - (Dun mor) - Big fort

Sometimes you have to ask their
Whereabouts. A bent figure, in a hamlet
Of three houses and a barn, will point
Towards the field. You will find them there,
Aloof lean markers, erect in mud.

Old Cross, Ardboe

Ardboe - (Achadh bho) - The hill of the cow

Ancient Celtic Christian sites stand today as a testimony to the dedicated prayer of the past.
Ardboe Old Cross is a 10th Century High Cross.

Fare ye well my lovely green clad hills
Farewell ye well my shamrocks green
Ye verdant banks of sweet Lough Neagh
And your silvery winding streams
Though far from home in green Tyrone
Too far from you I've strayed
I adore you Killcolpy
Where I spent my childhood days

Polly Devlin, Ardboe - Author, Journalist, Broadcaster and Film-maker.
Tom Mc Gurk, Brocagh - Journalist, Broadcaster.
Frank Mc Guigan, Ardboe - Legendary Gaelic footballer.
Patsy Forbes - Legendary Gaelic Footballer

"The Cross of Ardboe is elaborately carved with Twenty Two Scriptural scenes".

Close by the Cross there are also the remains of a church and an abbey. The abbey was founded by St Colman in 590 and the church is believed to have been built in the 16th century. These now stand in the graveyard.

Go to the Land
Whose love gives thee no rest.

by St Colman

Matt Quinn, Margaret O'Hagan (daughter) and Peggy Quinn

Derryloran Old Church and Graveyard, Cookstown

Derryloran - (Doire ua Lorain) - Loran's oak wood

Built from hewn stone in Gothic style, with a pinnacle tower, plain spire and vaulted vestibule.

Built in 1622 replacing an old church on the same site,200 years later a new church was built.
The present church was restored in 1862.Some of the graves date back to the late 17th century.

MAKE a little time for God,
As your rushing through the day,
Make a little time for him,
He will help you on your way,

Make a little time to care,
In the midst of all you do,
Sending many healing thoughts,
To people needing you,

Make a little time for God,
Just a little time to pray,
Care about your fellow man,
You can make a better day.

Altamuskin Mass Rock

Altamuskin, Ballygawley

Penal Rock, Altamuskin

A crude stone oratory, carved by a cousin,
Commemorates the place. For two hundred years
People of our name have sheltered in this glen
But now all have left. A few flowers
Wither on the alter, so I melt a ball of snow
From the hedge into rusty tin before I go.

John Montague

Seen here at Altamuskin Mass Rock, Mr Micky Harte (Manager of Tyrone Gaelic football team 2002-2007). Long ago people had to cross the hills to an almost inaccessible glen in Altamuskin for mass, called to this day "Glen-a-Haltra". The present site was refurbished circa 1952 by Mr Tom Montague. It is now looked after by an "Altar Glen Committee"
Mickey Harte and Brendan Burns - Pictured

Gort an Dara Mass Rock, Pomeroy

Gortindarragh - (Gort an dara) - Little field of the oak

People travelled from the surrounding townlands Shanmaghery, Camaghy, Largalea, Altmore, Galbally, Gortindarragh, Gortavoy, Glenbeg, Glenburisk, Kilmore, Kerrib etc to attend mass in the glen during the Penal days.

God bless the glens of Ireland,
Every rock and mountain pass,
'Twas those same glens under God
Preserved to us the Mass.
And if the day should come again
When Ireland calls for men,
She will not find them wanting
By the Mass rock in the glen.

by Felix Kearney

Other mass rocks in the county are in Omagh, Carrickmore, Broughderg, Sixmilecross and Dromore.

Brefni House, Creenagh, Killyman

Killyman - (Coill na meatha) - Wood of the saplings

A niche in the wall discovered during recent renovations in O'Rourke's house is said to have been used to hold the sacred vessels in Fr Roger Phelan's time (1673-1735) when mass was said in this house during the penal days. A set of tongs for making altar breads belonging to him is now in the Maynooth College Museum.

In the days before the motorcar every person passing over Verner's Bridge in Killyman had to pay a toll. There was one notable exemption. All persons going or coming from devine Services on a Sunday between 10 .00am and 3.00pm were exempt.

One famous son of the Killyman area is Primate Joseph Dixon born 1806 in Creenagh. Ordained in Maynooth in 1629 and was Archbishop of Armagh from 1852 - 1866.

Rev Joseph Gates S J was born in Drumkee in 1887 He was ordained at Milltown Park, Dublin 1921. He was a noted writer and author of several booklets published by the Irish Messenger Office. He died in Sydney 1947. Patsy and Phyllis O'Rourke - Pictured

Ballyrenan Portal Tomb, Newtownstewart

"Built as a grave for an ancient Irish Chief about 3000BC"

A series of tombs dating from the Neolithic period are at Ballyrenan between Drumquin and Newtownstewart.

Pheasants Roosting

Baronscourt, Newtownstewart

Tullyhogue Fort, Cookstown

Tullyhogue - (Telach Og) - Hill of Youth

It is at this fort the O'Neills were inaugurated.

Blessed Patrick O'Loughran, was a priest of Armagh diocese
and chaplain to the O'Neill's of Tyrone, he died in 1612.

While moonlight sleeps in the Glens of Tyrone
While clear burns croon through the night,
And the ghost of O'Neill steals back from Rome
To walk — where he needs no sight.

Donaghrisk, a circular walled graveyard close by, is the traditional burial place of the O'Hagans
who were residents here and responsible for the O'Neills' inaugurations.

Barrickstown House, Altmore

Ruins of Barrickstown House-Former barracks built in 1703
to curtail the activities of Shane Bernard O'Donnelly (1651-1716),
Crosscavanagh, Galbally. Son of Patrick Modder O'Donnelly.

"Fear not, fear not, sweetheart", he cried,
"Fear not the foe for me";
No chain shall fall whate'er betide,
On the arm that shall be free.

So leave your kin and come with me,
When the lark is in the sky;
And its with my gun I'll guard you,
On the mountains of Pomeroy.

Toothless Shane from Tyrone - "The Highway Man" "The Rapparee"
He was a terror to the authorities in Altmore.

Ms Margaret Quinn

"One of our former primary school teachers at St Mary's Pomeroy had a wealth of knowledge intended to guide us along life's way"

This teacher is a very special person
Who used her creativity
And loving,inquiring mind
To develop the rare talent
Of encouraging pupils to think,
To dream ,to learn, to try,to do.

Cuthbert Donnelly, Aughnacloy

"On his farm near Aughnacloy, September 2006 with the
Sam Maguire Cup - Getting a breath of fresh air"

Thank God for the happy sunbeams
Mellowing glen and brae,
Thank God for the light and sweetness
Of that September day,

by Rose Kavanagh

"Farewell old friend until we meet again" - Good bye Sam

Barnes Gap

Barnes Gap - (Bearnas Gap) - The Cap

A spectacular cleavage in the rugged scenery

A Mountain in Tyrone

When the summer comes to Ireland and the heather blooms again,
When the mountain - top becomes a misty blue.
The scent from bog and mireland brings memories in its train,
And I see again the scenes my boyhood knew.

The man who loves the mountain has a love that aye shall last;
A pleasure and a treasure all his own.
And I ,tonight am happy with my memories of the past
Dreaming of a mountain in Tyrone.

by F Kearney

The Hillside Today

Not a charm can be missed from the earth or the sky,
Yet the change is to deep for the ear or the eye,
And the roofless old walls in the valley below
To my heart are a picture of desolate woe;
Ah! the maiden's soft voice might be singing here still,
And her father's tall form be at work on the hill;
But- the homestead is empty, old and young are away,
And I'm standing alone on the hillside to-day.

by Rose Kavanagh

Millions of Irish people emigrated to North America, Australia and New Zealand in the eighteenth and nineteenth centuries.

The hills above Drumquin

Drumquin - (Droim Caoin) - Pleasant ridge

Drumquin has a rich and varied historical legacy with
a Neolithic stone circle, a Holy Well, and the Giant's Stone on Doolish Mountain.

Drumquin you're not a city but you're all the world to me
Your lot I would not pity should you never greater be
For I love you as I knew you when from school I used to run
On my homeward journey through you to the Hills above Drumquin.

I have seen the Scottish highlands ,they have beauties wild and grand
I have journed in the Lowlands, 'tis a cold and cheerless land
But I always toiled content for when each hard day 's work was done
My heart went back to the Hills above Drumquin.

When the whins across Drumbarley makes the fields a yellow blaze:
When the heather turns to purple on my native Dressog braes;
When the sandstone rocks of Claramore are glistening in the sun
Then nature's at her grandest on the Hills above Drumquin.

by Felix Kearney

Felix Kearney born In Drumquin 1889 was a renowned musician, poet and story teller.
...this is my native place…

Dr Seamus O Cathain from Drumquin is professor in the Irish folklore department in the University College Dublin and author of numerous books.

An Autumn Day in The Sperrins

The heather, O! the heather!
I would that I could sing
A little song of welcome
To the wondrous lovely thing.
I would bless the ruddy blossoms
Drinking in the noonday sun,
I would kiss the tiny leaflets
When the autumn day is done-
And the sunshine has departed,
For the dew has come instead,
Like a tender benediction
On a tired human head.

by Rose Kavanagh

Cookstown

Cookstown - (Cor a criche) - Round hill of the boundary

A picturesque location, backed by Slieve Gallion hills.
"A town with one of the longest streets in Ireland."

Slieve Gallion Brae

As I went out one morning all in the month of May
To view all your mountains and valleys so gay,
I was thinking of the flowers all a-going to decay
That bloom around you, bonny, bonny Slieve Gallen Braes.
Full oftimes I have wandered with my dog and my gun,
To view all your mountains and your valleys for fun,
But those days they now are gone, and I am far away,
So farewell unto you bonny, bonny, Slieve Gallen Braes.

The Holy Trinity Chapel, Cookstown

Bernadette McAlliskey Civil Rights activist and humanist hails from Cookstown.
Home to Barney Eastwood, former Gaelic football hero and Boxing Promoter.

Monastic Ruin, Killeter
Killeter - (Coill Iochtair) - Lower Wood
Magherakeel, (the plain of the Church), Killeter

I am of Ireland
And of the holy land of Ireland
Good sir I pray of ye
For saintly charity
Come dance with me
In Ireland.

14th Century Irish Poet

Ruins of St. Caireall's church and adjoining graveyard dating from around the 16th century.
The Magherakeel Monastic Site is one of Ireland's most important ecclesiastical centres

St Patrick's Well, Killeter
Killeter - (Coil lochtair) - Lower wood
Situated along the ancient pilgrimage trail to Lough Derg

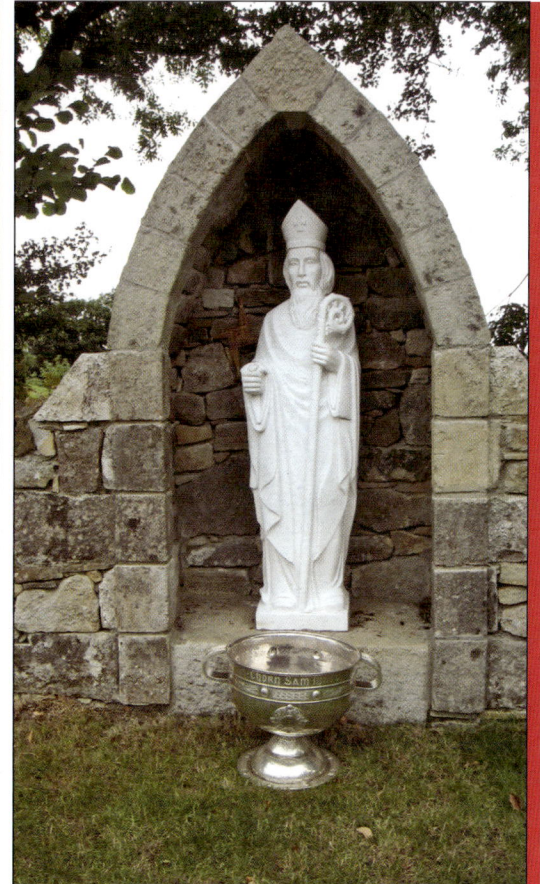

According to tradition St Patrick stopped here to rest himself and quench his thirst on returning from a period of Lenten Penitential Service on the nearby island Lough Derg. Many within the local community celebrate this event each year on St Patrick's day

May the love and protection
St Patrick can give
Be yours in abundance
As long as you live.

A holy well is located on the Irvinestown road in Dromore and also Tober Patrick (St. Patrick's Well) near Castlederg.

Mountjoy Castle, Brocagh

Overlooking Lough Neagh

Built in 1602

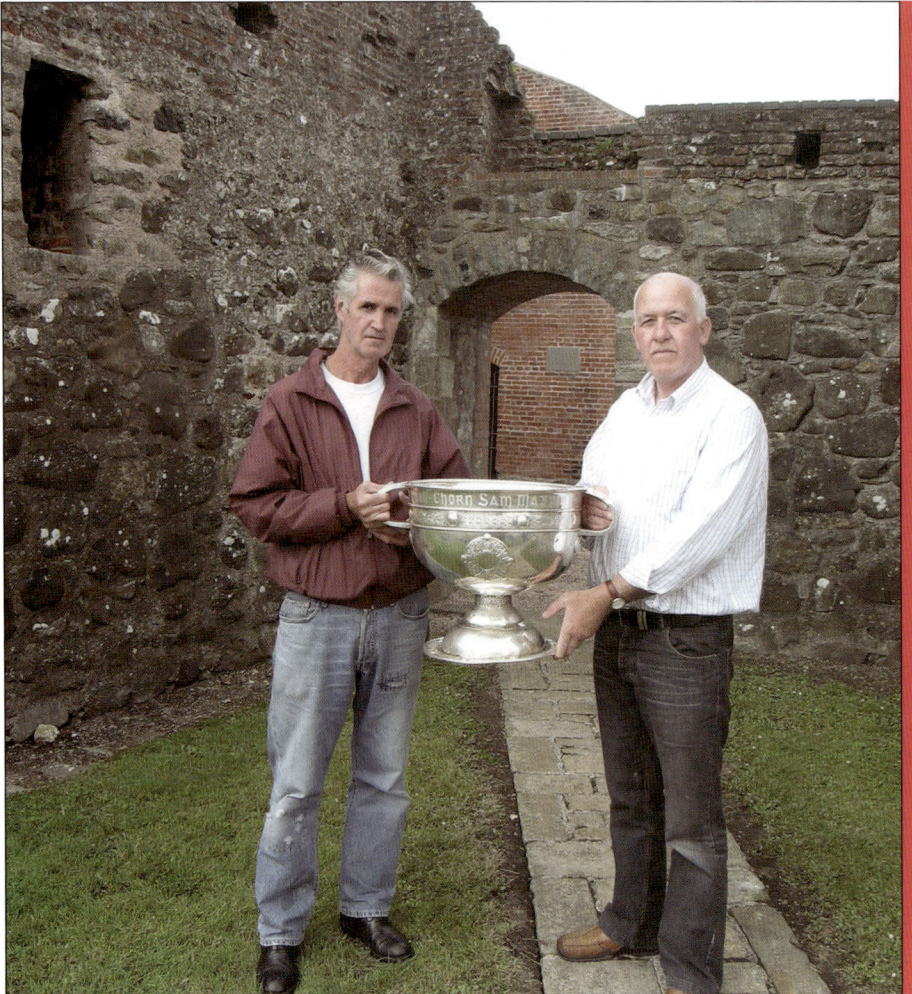

An Evenings Landscape

Moonlight pale
Paints the vale,
And in Fancy's ear,
Sad spirit —lays
Chant the memories of old hero days

by James Clarence Mangan

Waterfall at Canal near Coalisland
Coalisland - (Oilean a Ghuail)

Date of opening - 1787
Date of Abandonment - 1954

Cornmill Heritage Centre - provides insight, through exhibits and audio-visual shows, into the development of the Coalisland area over the past 3 centuries. The name Coalisland is derived from the fact that the area was subjected to an era of 'coal rush' when coal mining flourished. | Birthplace of Dennis Taylor and world champion snooker player. | Jody O'Neill the first senior football player to lead the Tyrone Gaelic team into an all Ireland semi final in 1956 was born in Coalisland.
Shauna Harte - Pictured

89

Cycling in the Sperrins

Were you ever in Tyrone, where the hills are so sunny and green
And the heather on the Sperrins looking down so proudly
"Tis there you would see more beauty in all this wide world. -
God bless you my sweet Tyrone, for where could your match be found.

Another Tyrone writer of Irish in modern times from Rouskey was An-tAthair Breandan O'Doibhlin,
professor of modern languages in Saint Patrick's College, Maynooth.

Sperrin Heritage Centre, Cranagh, Plumbridge

Cranagh - (Crannach) - A place abounding in trees

'Treasure of the Sperrins'

The Lord he made the Sperrins
The heather hills of Sperrins,

by W.F. Marshall

Plumbridge - "A mountain village at the foot of the Glenelly Valley" - "A place of beauty "

Sperrin Hillside Cottage

At Home upon the Bray

The House is still there standing
The walls maybe not as white
The Porch has gone a misssing
But it is still a prretty site

by Gerald Ferris

Gray's Printing Press, Strabane

Strabane - (Srath ban) - White holm

A small printing museum

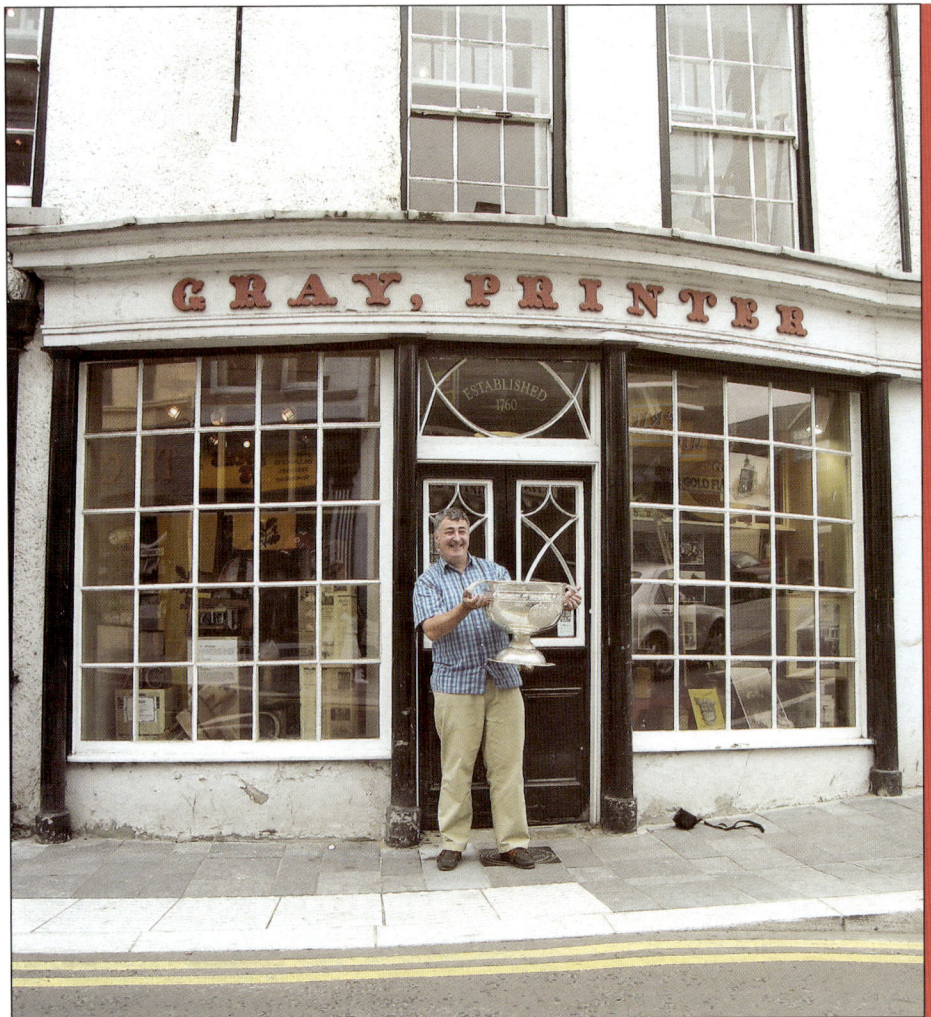

I have oft-times been in phoenix park aya and in Killarney fair
Or in blythe and bonny Scotland on the winding banks of Ayr
But yet in all my travels I have never met the one
That I could compare with Martha the flower of sweet Strabane

John Dunlap emigrated from this area, and moved to Pennsylvania . He printed the first copies of the
American Declaration of Independence, and published the first daily newspaper, the Pennsylvanian Packet in 1776.

The shop front has remained unchanged since the 18th century and inside the printing press room there are exhibits
and audio-visual shows outlining the role played by John Dunlap in the printing of the independence declaration.

One of Strabane's most famous sons Brian O'Nolan became more famous under the pen-names of Myles na Gopaleen and Flann O'Brien.
Brendan Gormley - Pictured.

River Derg

Running through Newtownstewart

President Wilson's Ancestral Home

Strabane - (Srath ban) - White holm

Dergalt, Strabane

We grow great by dreams. All big men are dreamers. They say things in the soft haze of a spring day or in the red fire of a long winters evening. Some of us let these great dreamers die, but others nourish and protect them.

by Woodrow Wilson

This thached white-washed house is on the slopes of the sperrins.

"This thatched white-washed house on the slopes of the Sperrins"
Woodrow Wilson - 28th US President (1913-1921)

Woodrow Wilson was a conservative idealist ,a fine orator and winner of the noble peace prize. He was also self —righteous and could be irritable!

This thatched white washed house, on the slopes of the Sperrin mountains, was his grandfather's home and contained some of the original furniture. The tiny outshot bed (sleeping nook) in the kitchen was close to the fire, where cooking pots and kettles still hang. The main room has larger curtain beds and a fine portrait of Judge James Wilson, the president's grandfather ,hanging over the fireplace .

James Wilson left this house for America in 1807 when he was 20 . The Wilsons still occupy the modern farmhouse next door and are full of stories about the fascinating Wilson photographs and artifacts.

Cecil Frances Alexander was born in Dublin in 1818. Frances moved with her family from Dublin to Strabane in 1833 when she was 15. She became involved in charity work and helping the local children and the poor. It was during her time in Strabane that she penned three of her best known hymns, 'There is a Green Hill Far Away', 'Once in Royal David's City' and 'All things Bright And Beautiful'.

Mullaghclogha in Glenelly is the highest point in Tyrone.
Magheramason is the lowest point in Tyrone.

Carleton's Cottage, Clogher

Clogher - (Clochar) - Stone place

A visit to Clogher valley, 'Carleton's Country'

My Own Country.

Pure was the breeze that fanned my cheek
As o'er Knockmanny's brow I went;
When every lonely dell could speak
In airy music vision-sent.
False world, I hate thy cares and thee,
I hate the treacherous haunts of men,
Give back my early life to me,
Give back to me my mountain glen.

By William Carleton.

William Carleton (1794- 1869), nineteenth century poet and novelist.
The Clogher Valley man was born at Prelisk, near Clogher and considered to be Ireland's greatest novelist.

Errigal Kerrogue view over the Clogher Valley

Lough Fea, Cookstown

Cookstown - (Cor a criche) - Round hill of the boundary

Across the black lake
Two figures row their boat
With slow, leaning strokes.
The grind of their rowlocks
In rhythmic as a heartbeat.

by John Montague

Drum Manor Forest Park

Cookstown
"Walk this way"

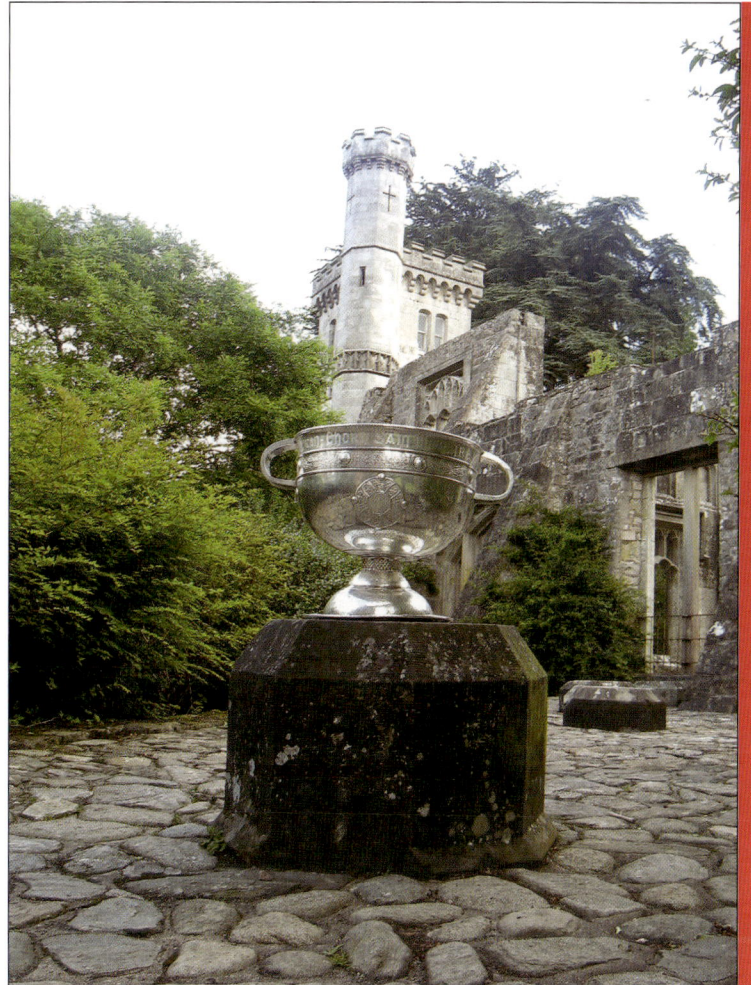

Its good to get away from noise,
From chaos and from Din,
To seek in solitude and peace
The beauty that's within.
To go into a quiet wood
And breathe its loveliness,
To contemplate in silence
Those things which calm and bless.

By Kathleen Gillum

Dunmisk Enclosure, Carrickmore

Carrickmore - (An Charraig Mhor) - Big Rock

More than 500 graves were found here.

'Tis idle- wil exhaust and squander
The glittering mind of thought in rain;
All —baffled reason cannot wander
Beyond her chain.

The floods of life runs dark —dark clouds
Make lampless night around its shore
The dead, where are they? in their shrouds
Man knows no more!

No more ,no more ;-
With aching brow
And restless heart,
And burning brain,
We ask, the When, the Where, the How,
And ask in vain.

by James Clarence Mangan

It sits on the brow of a gravel ridge overlooking the Camowen valley. Excavated in the mid-1980s. More than 500 graves were found, as well as the foundation trench for a rectangular timber building, probably a church. Excavation also provided evidence for glass making and iron-smelting. This site was probably used by an Early Christian monastic community.

Tulnacross Standing Stones, Cookstown

Tulnacross - (Tulach na croise) - Hill of the cross

"A pair of standing stones"

*In a green meadow
not far from town
stand ancient stones
that do not assume,
but cast their peace
to the earth below in a rain of yellow pansies
and call us to them with their inevitability,
Saying
'Friend, those who put us here
Knew you would come.'*

Sometimes they keep their privacy
In public places: nameless slender slabs
Disguised as gate-posts in a hedge ; and some,
For centuries on duty as scratching posts,
Are screened by ponies on blank uplands.

Mullaslin Limekill, Carrickmore

Mullaslin - the slatery summit

The area of Mullaslin townland is 2372 acres and abound with many old Gaelic placenames. It consist of a series of low rounded sand hills. The principal peaks are Binmore - the biggest peak, Crocknashinnagh - the hill of the fox and Crockancor - the rounded hill.

Mr James Ward, a champion whistler who broadcast many times on radio in the 1940's was from this area.

Mullaslin Rath, Carrickmore

Built on a small sandy hill overlooking the Camowen river valley

It consists of a roughly oval central area surrounded by two substantial earthen banks and ditches. A rath was an enclosed farmstead of the prosperous farmers and aristocracy of the early Christian period. Most raths have only one enclosing bank and ditch, so the presence of two at this site indicates it was built by people of high status.

Clogherny Ring fort in Mullaslin. Early farmers settled here and built fortifications for themselves and their animals

County Tyrone - All Ireland Champions

Senior Gaelic Football Final Croke Park 2005

Proud Brian Dooher (Captain) lifts the Sam Maguire Cup

The glory
Is not in never falling,
But in rising every time
You fall.

Peter Canavan

Peter Canavan is arguably one of the greatest gaelic footballers that has ever graced the playing fields of Ireland; oft times referred to as "Peter the Great"

Hold on,
Hold Fast,
Hold out,
Patience is Genius.

U.S. Grant's Ancestral Homestead

Dergenagh, Dungannon

18th President of the United States (1869-1877)

The great grandfather of Ulysses Simpson Grant, 18th President of the USA, was born here in 1738 and emigrated to America in 1760.

" Give me your impoverished and I will feed them"

" The land of the free and the home of the brave"

It was here that the maternal ancestors of Ulysses Simpson Grant, the victorious commander of the Union forces during the Civil War and 18th President of the United States (1869-1877) raised their families, tended their animals and harvested their crops.

Adjoining visitor centre - tells the full Grant story and has interesting exhibits of rural life and audio-visual theatre.

"Content in my cottage"

Oh, the old turf fire!
What a welcome now it brings.
As the crickets chirrup lively,
And the kettle starts to sing;
And we all join in the chorus'
With a merry lilting song'
To welcome neighbours "droppin' in"
And join the happy throng.

Moymore Stone Circle, Pomeroy

Moymore - (Magh mor) - The great plain.

Sweet Pomeroy

Last Easter Sunday as I sat and pondered
Oe'r days and scenes I shall see no more
Sweet youthful days when I used to wander
From Cornamaddy to Carrickmore
Though many a city since then I have been in
New York, Chicago, Fort Wayne and Troy
My heart still pines for your fields Killeenan
My bosom yearns for you sweet Pomeroy.

by P.J.Fox aka Phelim O'Dowd

Close to Moymore stone circles there is a Rath and a Ring Barrow (burial mound).
Raths (Ringforts) were built in the lowlands to house an extended farming family and some livestock in the early Christian times (AD500-1200).

Murnell's Portal Tomb, Pomeroy
Murnells - (Murtha Neill) - O'Neill's Mounds

Search out the furthest ones, slog on
Through bog, bracken, bramble: arrive
At short granite footings in a plan.

Tromague - (Tromog) - Little elder tree.
In 1981 excavations took place on Con O'Neill's land in Tromague, Pomeroy. A cist (clay pot) was found containing the bones of a young girl.
A lunar (crown) used in the reign of the O'Neills was found .It is now in the National museum, Dublin.

Fintona

Fintona - (Fionntamnach) - A fair coloured field

Donacavey church ruin and graveyard

Donaghavey - (domhnach a chabha) - the church of the hollow

Some remains of the old church that stood here in 1622, are all that remain today.
On the left hand side of the lane leaving the church, are the remains of a medieval celtic cross.
Only the short but decorative cross-shaft survives known locally as St Patrick's cross.

I'm not afraid of death or the stoppage of breath,
But some silly notions come into my head.
I would like quite a lot to know in what spot
My kinfolk will dibble me after I'm dead.

by Felix Kearney

It is believed locally that St Patrick was the founder of the first Christain church here. This site, no longer lies in a hollow, most likely due to centuries of burials and church constructions, as it now commands a view over the surrounding countryside from its lofty position.

Drumragh old church and graveyard

Omagh - (Omaigh) - Sacred place

Burial place of the great poetress Alice Milligan (1865-1953)
Nior char si aon tir ach Eire
She loved no other country, but Ireland.

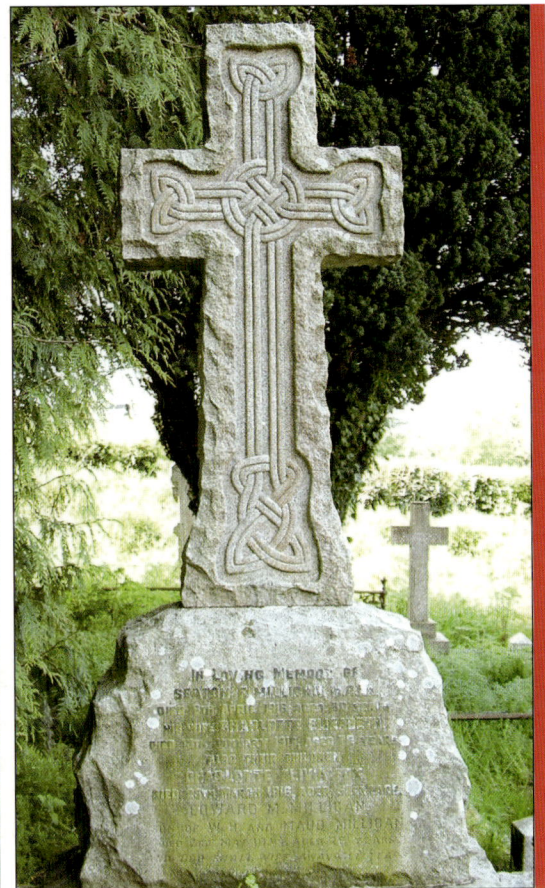

Here she sleeps her long lost sleep, midst those who were her own,
Green her memory we shall keep, forever in Tyrone.
Her stainless soul has found its goal, and gained eternal rest,
And will surely meet with others who loved Ireland the best

by Felix Kearney

Boughal Brague, Camaghy, Pomeroy

Camaghy - (Cam achadh) - The crooked field

The stone to mark the place where bodies were buried during Neolithic times

And here, four thousand years ago
Gazed Neolithic eyes
On wonders older still.

Shanmaghery Neolithic Graveyard, Pomeroy

Shanmaghery - (Sean-Mhachairc) - The old plain

Good bye to the world

For now I leave you. Yonder trees
O'ershade the churchyard where I'll lie.
The longest of all voyages
Is here begun. So, World, good-bye!

by Donnchadh Mor O'Dalaigh

The Rock Pump, Rock, Cookstown

The Water Carrier

Twice daily I carried water from the spring,
Morning before leaving for school, and evening
Balanced as a fulcrum between two buckets.
A brambled - rough path ran to the river
Where you stepped carefully across slime - topped stones,
With corners abraded as bleakly white as bones.

by John Montaque

Sean Quinn and Anthony Quinn - Pictured.

Dredge Suspension Foot Bridge, Caledon

Caledon - (Ceannard) - High head

"Unique in Ireland"

An Creagan Visitor Centre, Creggan

Creggan - (-An Creagan) - Little crag

"Reflecting the past"

The Creggan White Hare

In the townland there lived a white Hare,
As swift as a swallow that flies through the air.
You may search through this world but find none to compare
With the pride of lower Creggan, our bony White Hare.

by John Graham

The An Creagan Visitor Centre provides information on archaeological and geological aspects of the county.

More than just a Holiday

An Clachan Self Catering Cottages

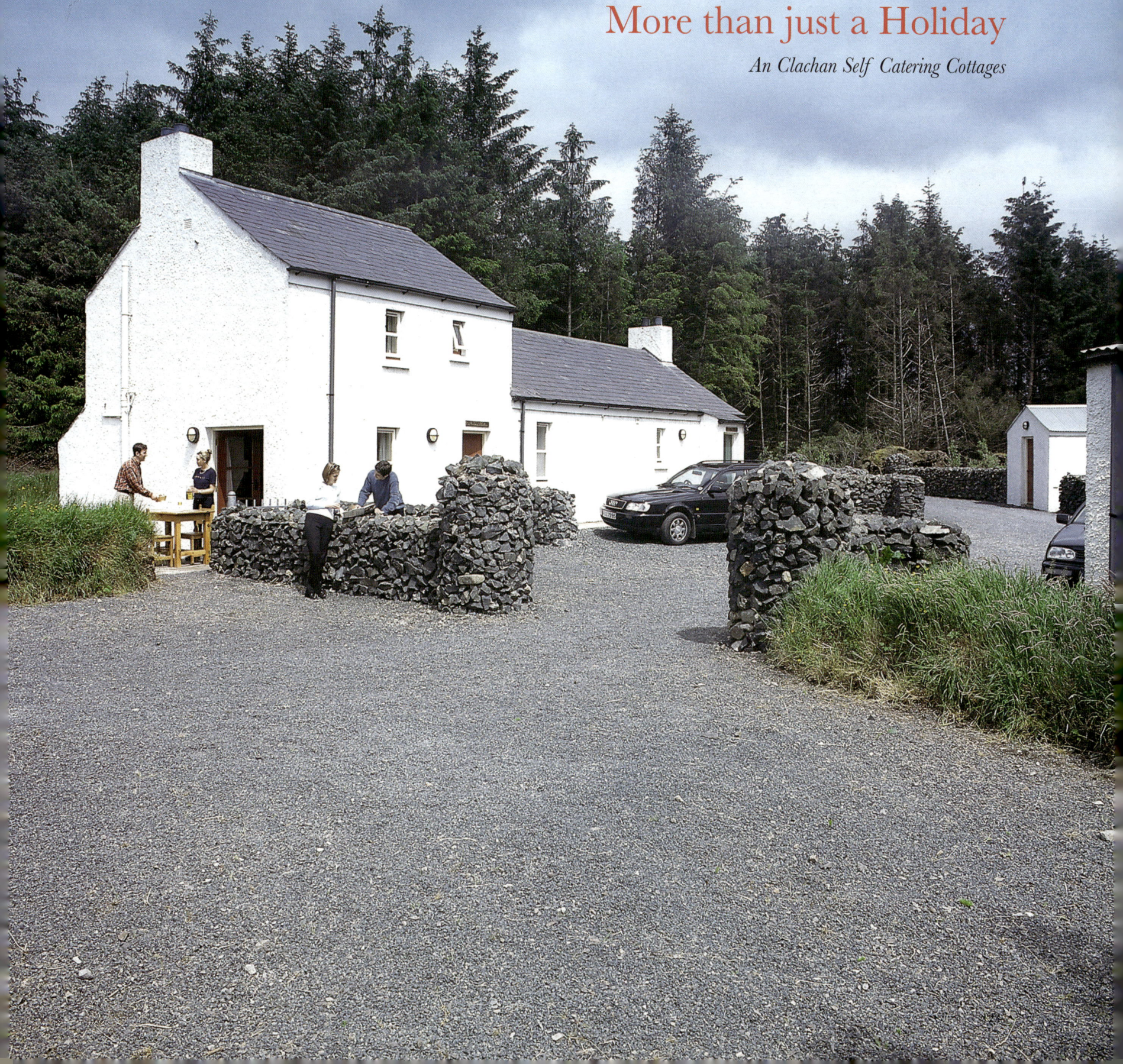

Loughmacrory Court Tomb, Loughmacrory, Carrickmore

Loughmacrory - (Loch mha Ruain) - Mac Ruain's Lake

Life is eternal and love is immortal…
And death is but a horizon and the
horizon is but the limit of our sight.

by Abraham Lincoln
(derived from a prayer by William Penn)

This is right by the road, so close in fact that a row of stones that may have been the facade to form the field boundary. | Nearest the road is a very narrow court. Beyond this is a ruined gallery. The cairn is around 25m long and stretches at right angles away from the road. At the far end is a hodge-podge of stones. A wall seems to have been constructed across where the far gallery should be and in front of that is a very disrupted court.

Loughmacrory Wedge Tomb
(Dermot and Grania's Bed)

Deep and tender peace and quiet
'Neath the fairy thorn lone,
From its ancient rath o'er looking
Half the glens of sweet Tyrone

by Rose Kavanagh

John Donaghy - Pictured

The Sperrins

The Sperrins

The glens and valleys are deep sided and warm
In spring the wind is green but yellow speckled and flecked
The black rivers give passage to little fish
In autumn the winds are burnished with orange
In winter the wind is white and grey
The black waters carry gold and tints of bog earth
In summer the wind is green: it is threaded with yellow and scarlet.

by Sam Burnside

Overlooking the Glenelly Valley

Those who share in summer's bounty,
Living close to natures beauty,
Need not travel far to find
Riches for the heart and mind.

Sweat houses were numerous in Glenelly but the sweat house in Fallagh Glen was best preserved.

Seskilgreen Passage Tomb, Aughnacloy

Seskilgreen - (Seisioch Chill Ghreine) - Plot of the church of the sun

Seskilgreen

A circle of stones
surviving behind a
guttery farm house,

the capstone phallic
in a thirsty meadow:
Seskilgreen Passage Grave.

Cup, circle
Triangle beating
their secret dance

(eyes, breasts,
thighs of a still
fragrant goddness).

I came last in May
to find the mount
drowned in bluebells

with a fearless wren
hoarding speckled eggs
in a stony crevice

by John Montague

Castle Caulfield

St Oliver Plunkett is known to have visited the castle in 1670

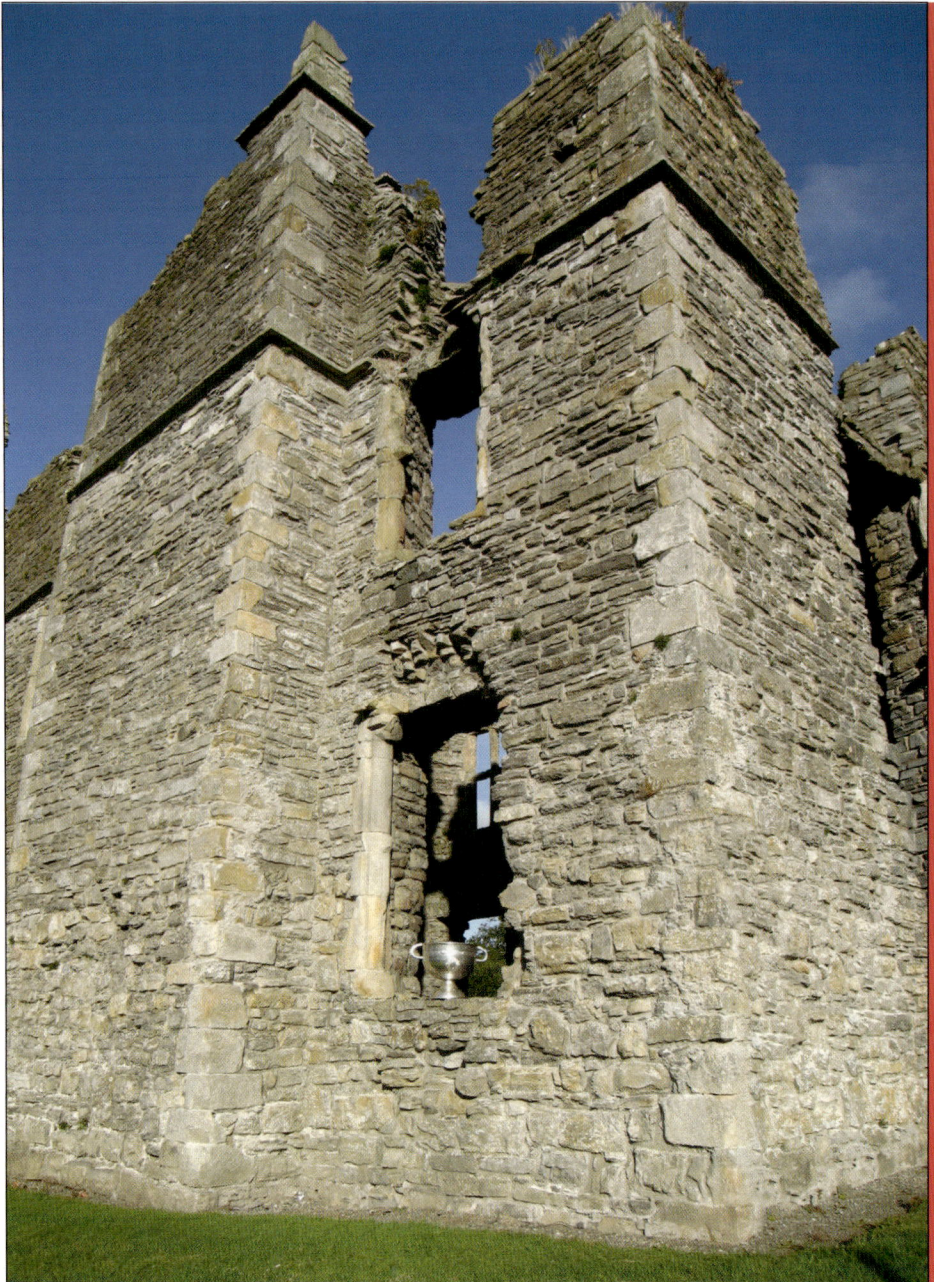

But night soon
Brings the moon,
And no more the golden sunset falls
Over Castlecaufield ruined castle.

White Deer

Parkanaur, Castlecaufield

At times we can but stand and gaze
In awe at Nature's majesty.
So it has been since earlier days
And to the end of time will be.

Harry Avery's Castle, Newtownstewart

14th Century Gaelic Stone Castle

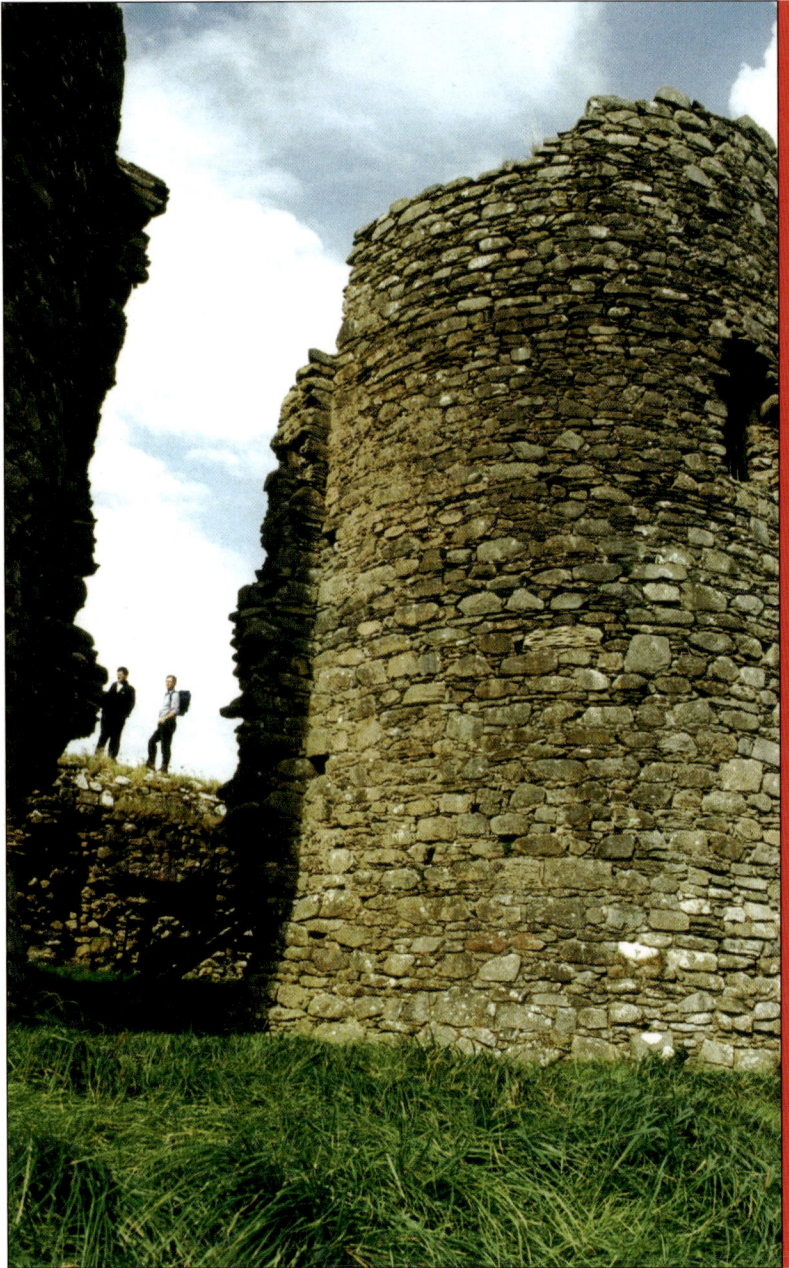

Newtownstewart provides the setting for the majestic ruins of the gaelic stronghold of the O' Neill's. Although traditionally associated with Henry Aimbreidh O' Neill who died in 1392 it is not certain whether it dates from the 14th century or 15th century. It is an unusual and interesting structure and especially important in relation to the study of native Irish medieval life prior to the plantation period.

The castle consisted originally of a two story rectangular construction fronted by it's most visible remaining features - a pair of D shaped towers. Other surviving attributes include a draw bar slot for the main door, a latrine chute and marks of wicker centring in the tower vaults.

Stewart Castle, Newtownstewart

"A castle of lime and stone of good strength, 4 stories high" - built in 1619.
Excavations conducted on site in 1999 uncovered 4 large burnt posts from the doorway.
Stewart Castle has also the distinction of being the site of a significant Bronze Age
discovery; an intact double cist grave and capstone. The grave contains two decorated
vessels lying adjacent to cremated remains approx 4,000 years old.

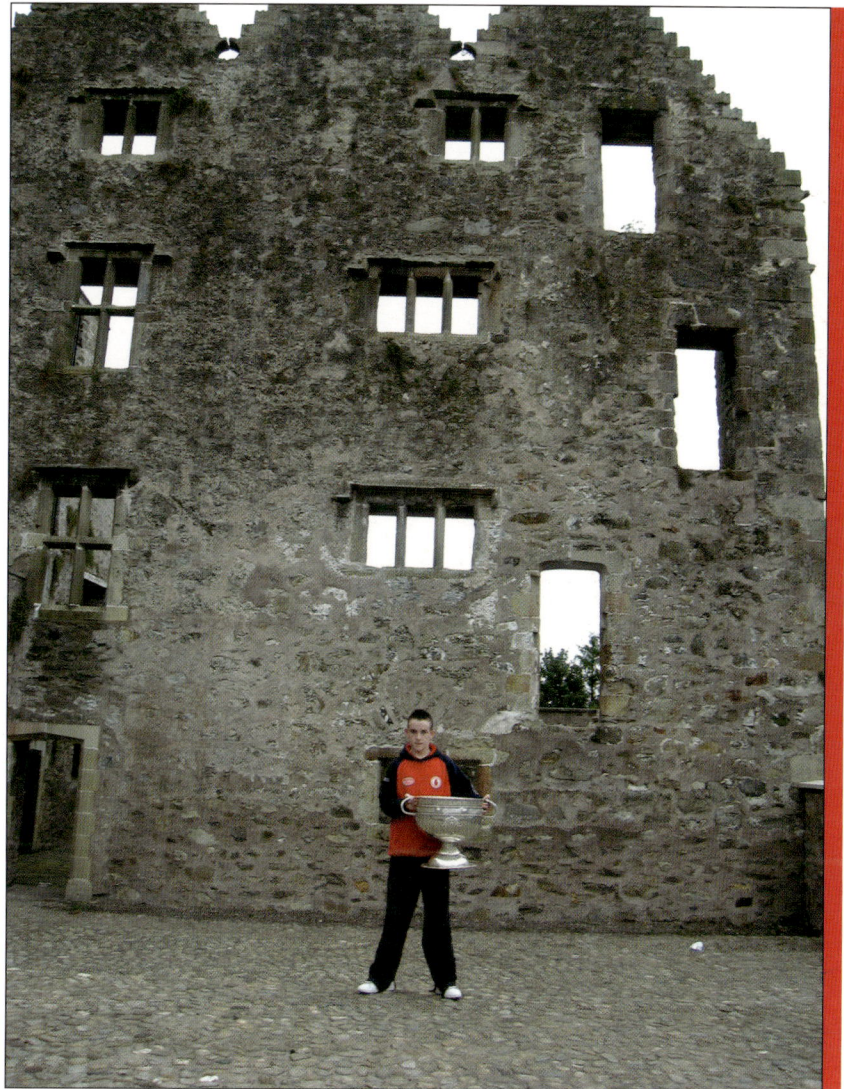

The pillar towers of castles, how wondrously they stand
By the lakes and rushing rivers through the valleys of our land
In mystic file, through the isle they left their heads sublime,
These grey old pillar temples, these conquerors of time!.

by Denis McCarty, Irish Poet (1817 - 1882)

Sean McNamee - Pictured

Relignaman Womens's Graveyard

in a townland formely known as Killeen Carrickmore

Where no living woman or dead man should enter

The name Relignaman comes from the Irish, Relig na mban. The graveyard is a small, sub-rectangular enclosure, c 19m across, surrounded by a grass covered stony bank and dates from the early Chrisitan period.

I am blinded by the hair and my tears together
The dark night and rain come down on me together.

by James Clarence Mangan

Dún Ruadh (3000BC - 1500BC), Crock

Greencastle - (Caislean glas)

Dún Ruadh - (The Red Citadel) - The Red Fort
A magnificent site of immense importance. First excavated in the early 1930's, it is a henge
but it also was an earlier Neolithic site which was occupied until the early bronze age.

A Multiple-kist Cairn and Henge
(3000BC -1500BC)

Sacred Trees

No murd'ring Axes let 'em feel,
Nor violate the Groves with impious Steel;
From rude Assaults and Force prophane forbear,
Avenging Deities inhabit there.

by R.Rapin De Hortorum (1665)

The parish of Greencastle was formed in 1892
An Irish college was founded in Greencastle Co Tyrone in 1911

Shane Barnagh, Altmore

The Lost Tradition

The heathery gap where the Rapparee,
Shane Barnagh, saw his brother die-
On a summer's day the dying sun
Stained its colours to crimsom:
So breaks the heart, Brish-mo-Cree.

by John Montague

James Sheilds one of Abraham Lincon's generals in the American Civil War was born on December 12th 1806 in Altmore, near Cappagh.

James Shields (1806-1879), Altmore, Pomeroy

Altmore - (Alt mor) - Big glen

"From the green fields of Ireland to the purple plains of Illinois"

James Shields one of Abraham Lincoln's generals in the American Civil War was born in Altmore near Cappagh, close to Pomeroy. James Shields, soldier, jurist and Statesman of Mexican and American civil war fame described by historians as: (The greatest Irishman who ever trod American soil).

His professional and legislative career was unique. He was in turn a teacher, lawyer, legislator, state auditor, land commissioner, State Governor, lecturer, landowner and judge of the Supreme Court. He still holds the unique honour of representing three different states as a Senator.

James Sheilds lived close to the Altmore Hotel - Pictured

Dromore old Church and Graveyard -17th century

Dromore - (Droim mor) - The great ridge

The grave

The grave, it is deep and soundless,
And canopied over with clouds;
And trackless and dim and boundless
Is the unknown land that it shrouds.

by James Clarence Mangan

Archeological features of Dromore Old Church were discovered below the surface.
The most obvious were skeletons and a large grave slab dated 1670's which may relate to a family who lived in Trillick.
At the base of the promonotory below the church is a spring, known locally as the "Eye Well"
There were a number of ancient earthen forts in the Dromore area.
At Dullaghan is a Druid's Altar - a small roof less chamber tomb

In Dromore a Cistercian Abbey is said to have been built on the site of an ancient nunnery
founded by Saint Patrick for Saint Cettumbria, the first Irish female who received the veil from his hands.
Also there was a friary in Dromore which housed the Franscians from 1637-1717.

Tyrone at the Dawning of the Day

Day Break

For one enchanted moment
The world seems fresh and new
Before the sunbeams break the spell
And dry the morning dew

Our Lady's Grotto, Pomeroy

On the site of the former St. Patricks Church

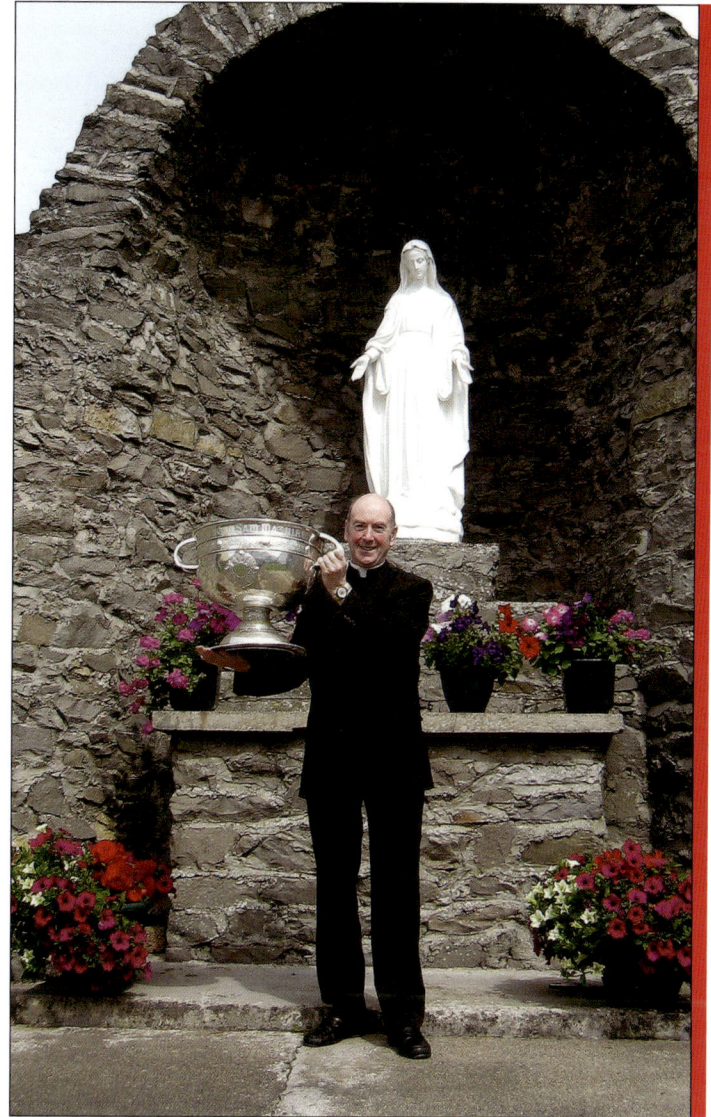

Christ be with me,
Christ be within me,
Christ behind me, Christ before me
Christ beside me, Christ to win me,
Christ to comfort me, christ above me,
Christ in quiet, christ in danger,
Christ in hearts of all that love me,
Christ in mouth of friend and stranger.

Monsignor Barney McAleer, Johannasburg, South Africa comes from Pomeroy.
Fr Martin McVeigh PP - Pictured

Winter in the Sperrins

Though Winter winds are blowing chill,
Our memories can warm us still,
And evenings have a special glow,
Outshining frost or fog or snow.
A time of friendship, love and cheer,
To carry with us through the year,
And soon we'll see dark days depart,
And springtime lift each waiting heart.

Corrick Abbey, Corickmore, Plumbridge.

The first religious use of the site may have been c.560
when St. Columba founded a monastery and centre of learning.

Now world, good-bye! I've done with you,
I go to better company
You broken blade and rusted through,
I'm weary of your trickery.

Now I must turn another way,
You battered world decayed and blind!
How great advantages 'twere this day
To leave this mouldy trunk behind!

To seek your paths no more and sleep
More sound than on the warmest feather!
Not for a time apart to keep,
Yet fear to lose you altogether!

I trod awhile the idle way,
Defiled my soul for worldly gain,
Awhile in mire I blindly lay,
Then sought the cleansing streams again.

By Donnchadh Mor O Dalaigh

Corac, where the Glenelly and Owenkillew rivers meet. Where the two rivers meet is known as 'the meeting of the waters'.

Later about 1465 Corrick Abbey was founded by the 3rd Order Regular Franciscan Friars. The Tertiaries or Third Order of St. Francis were a lay institute founded by St. Francis of Assisi five years before his death in 1226. The members of the Third Order Regular lived in monasteries or convents, but did not come into existence until after the death of Francis. These Franciscan brethrens were predominantly lay people who lived in the community while doing pastoral work in the surrounding parish. Sometimes there were schools attached to the monasteries. It is not known if there was a school at Corrick. The monastery ceased to be in use by 1603.

There were also Franciscan friaries at Pubble (Newtownstewart) and Scarvagherin (near Spamount), Co. Tyrone

Errigal Kerrogue Church and Bullaun Stone, Gort, Ballygawley

Errigal Kerrogue - (Earagail do chiarog) - Do Chairog's oratory

Ruined remains of a medieval church in a walled graveyard.
Built into the wall of the ruined church is a replica of an effigy of a male figure.

"Where clerics sing like birds"
St Adhamhnan

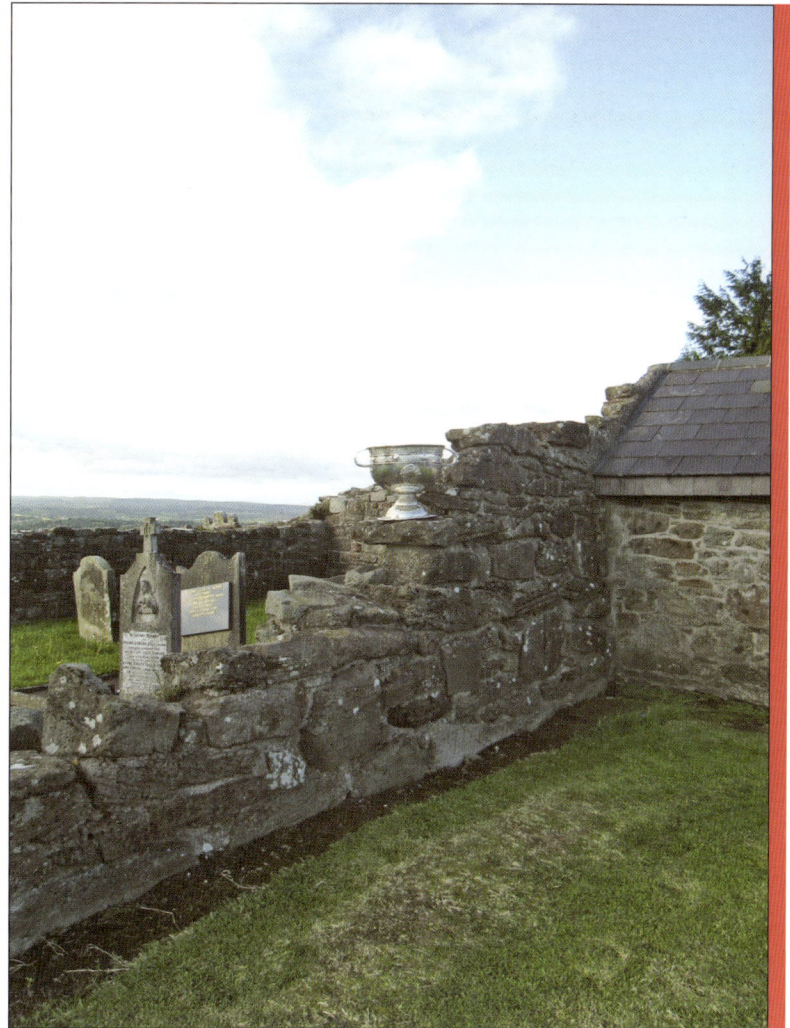

The mass is over, they have gone in peace
But wind flays the Church sides
I fear my frail cover will be blown
Despite the sunlight on confessional doors,
Desultory coins,
The urgent reaching of the woman's prayers.

His eminence the late Cardinal Mc Rory
and primate of all Ireland was born near Ballygawley

This early Christian site is believed to have been founded by Saint Adhamhnan [Onan] in the 7th century. St Adhamhnan held the position of Abbot of Iona after St Colmcille and wrote a biography of the saint. There is an adjacent structure which may have been a watchman's house, a rock cut souterrain in the field beyond the walled graveyard and a bullaun stone marking a possible ancient entrance to the church precincts. Excavation in 1935 revealed a number of chambers, passages and objects. The findings suggest that is was used as a refuge in times of danger and it is recorded that the church was attacked by Norse raiders in the ninth century. This ancient church site has St Ciaran as its patron saint.

The History Park, Omagh

Omagh - (Omaigh) - Sacred place

Open the door to the past, the story of the Irish settlement is told

The history park relates the human history of settlement in Ulster from the stone age (8000 BC) to the 17th century.

The Hinge of History

The hinge of history swings in all directions
As the happenings of the past are written down.
Out of all that has occurred since man's beginnings,
Less has been recorded than waits to be found.

Some have asked why must we study history;
It just encourages us to live in the past.
When we forget history we repeat its mistakes,
As the outcome of humanity is cast.

The Forestry, Pomeroy

Silent Peace

What peace lies in the forest
Beneath the oak and beech
A lesson learned in silence
These ancient trees can teach.

Within Pomeroy Forest there was a Forest Service and a Forestry School.
Gortavoy Bridge close to Pomeroy is known locally as the bridge with three horns,
the small river running through it actually negotiates through a bridge that is in three parts.

Main Street, Pomeroy

Pomeroy - (Cabhan an chaorthainn) - Round hill of the mountain ash

'A Village pearched on an elevation'
It is renowned as the village with the highest elevation in
Ulster and its railway station was the highest in Ireland.

The Mountains of Pomeroy

The morn as breaking bright and fair,
The lark sang in the sky,
When the maid she bound her golden hair,
With a blithe glance in her eye;
For, who beyond the gay green-wood,
Was a-waiting her with joy?
Oh, who but her gallant renardine,
On the mountains of Pomeroy.

by Dr George Sigerson

The grandfather of Colonel James Irwin, the Apollo 15 astronaut who was the first man to drive a lunar rover on the Moon in 1971,
was born in Pomeroy. The Irwins still have family connections in the area. | Blind fiddler and All Ireland Champion John Loughran came from Pomeroy.
Thomas Donnelly a former Irish Boxing Champion comes from Limehill, Pomerory. | Philomena Begley - the undisputed 'Queen' of Irish Country Music comes from Pomeroy.

Ulster-American Folk Park, Omagh

Omagh - (Omaigh) - Sacred place

An Emigration Studies Centre

Judge Thomas Mellon's Ancestral Homestead

Misty hills of home

Only those who know the longing of an exile's heart can tell
How fond memories become a thronging,
Of those scenes I loved so well.
Glens of bracken, gorse and rushes, far across the foam,
Dark Tyrone among the bushes, and the hills of home.

by Felix Kearney

The ancestral farmsteads and cottages of some of those people
who rose to positions of power in the united states have been preserved here in the American Folk Park.
Judge Thomas Mellon Cottage - Pictured.

The boyhood home of Archbishop John Hughes (1797-1864) has been relocated to the Ulster American Folk Park.
His birthplace was the parish of Truagh in the Clogher diocese.
He became Archbishop of New York, and founder of St Patrick's Cathedral on Fifth Avenue.
He was a politician and champion of the Irish Catholic immigrants. His cottage was moved into the park and rebuilt stone by stone.

Athenree Portal Tomb, Carrickmore

The Athenree Portal Tomb with its massive capstone

"Walls for the wind
And a roof for the rain."

156

Athenree Portal Tomb (Chambered Grave)

Or on a spring night in Bernish Glen when it is only

"Across the Gap
There's light to see
A lone crow flap
To Athenree".

by W.F. Marshall

The Athenree Portal Tomb is reputed to be one of the largest capstones on an Ulster portal tomb.
Close by to here is Copney stone circles.

Campa Chormaic Summer Camp, Brantry

Campa Cormac - (Campa Chormaic) - Camp Cormac

"Failte go Campa Chormaig"- The Brantry

Named after the great Cormac Mc Anallen

Brendan Mc Anallen's enthusiasm - "It's the breath in all things alive here at Campa Cormac"

There's music and there's laughter
With children at their play.

Clogher

Clogher - (Cloghar) - Stone structure

Clogher - "A quaint village in the heart of the Clogher Valley"

CLOGHER
7th CENTURY CROSS
CONSIDERED BY SOME
TO BE A SUNDIAL
WITH 3 PRAYER HOUR
DIVISIONS OF THE EARLY
CELTIC CHURCH
ORIGINAL INSIDE THE CATHEDRAL

"Insula Doctorum Et Sanctorum"
"The Island of Scholars and Saints"

by Donal O'Sullivan

St. Macartan's Cathedral, Clogher

Cathedral

Somewhere, under vaults and bosses,
between chantries and chapels,
undeterred by organ,
unfazed by glitter of glass,
in the heart of this storehouse of worship
is one pure silent note
the holiness of the everyday,
darkness cradling a star.

Clogher is a site of ancient importance in Ireland. In the 5th Century it was the Seat of the first Bishopric in Ireland.
The first Bishop was St. Macartan (buried in the cathedral grounds), was one of St. Patrick's disciples. The Cathedral is named in his honour.

Munderadoe Mass Garden and Hedge School

Magh an Doire Duibh - The plain of the black oak grove.

Pomeroy

I Still crouching 'neath the sheltering hedge,
Or stretched on mountain fern,
The teacher and his pupils met feloniously to learn.

by J. Walsh

Pictured from left to right: Pat Hagan, Damien Hagan, Felix Hagan and Columba Hagan.

The Mass Rock in the Glen

In a lonely mountain valley,
In the County of Tyrone,
Lies one of Ireland's hallowed spots.
Deserted and unknown.
But few who write historic tales
Or weild the poet's pen
Can say with pride, I knelt beside,
The Mass rock in the glen.

I am proud that I am mountain bred,
This is my native place;
Those mountain glens have always been
The stronghold of our race
'Twas here our fathers earned the right
To bear the name of men
When they kept the faith of Padraig
By the Mass rock in the Glen.

by Felix Kearney

There was once a Latin school in Turnabarson, Pomeroy

Wellbrook Beetling Mill

Kildress

A water-powered 18th century beetling mill

The Old Mill Wheel

The shadows of evening are falling,
The birds in the wildwood are still:
Comes the ghosts of old memories a calling
And my thoughts wonder back to the Mill.

The lilt of the lark in the morning,
The lover of nature may thrill,
But give me the old wheel a-turning
And sing me the song of the Mill.

by Felix Kearney

165

Overlooking the hills of Mullaghcairn, Carrickmore

Carrickmore - (An Carraig Mhor) - Big Rock

*The Landscape
is always with me
in my head, in my music.*

Enya

It was the Raffetys of Carrickmore who introduced Professor Eamonn O Tuathail of Trinity College Dublin to the native Irish speakers in the parish of Termonmaguirk and Lower Badoney when he was doing research there in 1929. | Traolach O Raifeartaigh from Carrickmore, one time secretary of Department of Education wrote an interesting book on Irish poetry Maighistri San Fbiliocht (1939) and contributed articles to several Gaelic journals.
The Gormley Family - Pictured

166

Old Churchyard, Carrickmore

Overlooking the village of Carrickmore is the smallest townland in Ireland
"Old Church Yard" at just over haf an acre.

A little lonely green graveyard,
The old church tower is solemn guard,
The gate with nought but sunbeams bared.

And quiet heart and bird and tree
Seem linked in some strange sympathy
Too fine for mortal eye to see.

by Rose Kavanagh

Dean Brian McGuirc was an 18th Century priest who was Dean of Armagh for 40 years and Vicar-General to St Oliver Plunkett. A hero of the penal days, he died in his ninetieth year in Armagh jail on 13th February 1713. The high school in the village is named after him.

Termonmaguirc Jubilee High Cross

Carrickmore - (An Carraig Mhor) - Big Rock

"They met constantly to hear the teaching of the apostles,
to share in community life, break bread and pray."

*In the name of the father
and of the son
and the holy spirit.
Amen.*

The raising of the Tearmann High Cross is a symbol of our Salvation, an appreciation of 2000 years of Christianity,
a tribute to Colmcille and a commendation to the people who for over fourteen hundred years have been disciples of Jesus Christ.

2000 Anno Domini
Jesus I trust in you. Body of Christ sanctify me.
A Iosa, ta muinin agam asat. A Chorp Chriost naomhaigh me.

St Colmcille's Chair

Mullinalap, Carrickmore

Mullinalap - A Sacred Place

In the winds that blow round Mullinalap
When the matins hour is nigh
Of old `tis said a chant was heard
A coming from out the sky
The prayer of the monks, who days gone by
Inspired by Colmcille
Did plant the faith, the cross and the mass
On that bleak and lonely hill
That mystic prayer, they say, did run
"All thanks to God who reigns on high
The seed we sowed lives on".

Cathaoir án tSolaís - Chair of solace

St Colmcille's Well, Mullinalap, Carrickmore

Beside the bed there's a knee-worn stone,
Where mothers' went to pray,
'May the spirit who breathed on Columba
The light and fire breathed by the spirit
In response to a mother's prayer
Moved many a son from hill and glen
Like Columba For God to dare.

Mullinalap, the rock on which is located the bed, well and chair place, is associated with St. Colmcille. On Mullinalap there is an atmosphere that is only experienced by visiting: a stillness and calming effect. The shadow of the rock rests gently on the holiest of places. A sense of history and sacredness seeps out from the rock protecting the Tearmann and there is an aura of peace in this area made holy by the Patron Saint, his monks and all those down the ages who came there to give praise and glory to God.

The Whispering River Strule, Omagh

Joe McMahon - Omagh - All Ireland Medalist 2005

Leave me a memory of Ireland, of springtime in Co Tyrone
The mist over valley and mireland, and a cottage that once was my own.
Let me picture the old town of Omagh, where I as a boy went to school
And lover's retreat where fond sweethearts still meet
By the whispering River Strule.

by Felix Kearney

Omagh - Number Ten, Michael Street.
It's said to be the smallest street, not just in Ulster, but in the whole of Ireland, for it is just one house long.
The Sacred Heart RC Church is notable for its distinct uneven spires
Benedict Kiely (1919-2007) famous novelist, writer, journalist and broadcaster, was born in Dromore and lived in Omagh from 1925-1950.
Brian Friel - Playwright - Omagh, Born 1929.

172

Loughry Portal Tomb, (The Giant's Grave 2000BC)

Loughry College, Desertcreat, Cookstown

Loughry - (Luachrai) - A place abounding in rushes
Desertcreat - (Diseart crioth) - Waste place
Burnt remains of bodies found in the early 1950's

And the grave where sleeps the giants
In the dewy pasture land,
Haunted by the weird traditions
Childhood did not understand.

Wander through deserted chambers,
Round the nurseries, up the stair,
Recollecting forms and faces
That can never meet me there.

Sometimes culling fragrant blossoms
From the wood, the stream beside,
Dropping them from weary fingers,
Sauntering home at eventide.

by Emmeline Lindsay

The Summer House of Dean Jonathan Swift's (1667–1745) is based on the grounds of Loughry College.
It was here that he penned some of his writings. He is famous for the book "Gulliver's Travels".

174

Bishop Patrick Donnelly - A penal bishop

Buried in Church of Ireland graveyard, Desertcreat

Went under the name Phelim Brady "The bard of Armagh"

The Bard of Armagh

Oh, list to the lay of a poor Irish harper
And scorn not the strains of his old withered hand
But remember his fingers they once could move sharper
To raise up the memory of his dear native land

At a fair or a wake I could twist my shillelagh
Or trip through a jig with my brogues bound with straw
And all the pretty colleens in the village or the valley
Loved their bold Phelim Brady, the bard of Armagh

Formil Standing Stone, Broughderg

Formil - (Formeal) - Round hill

The most common stone monument in Ireland is the standing stone

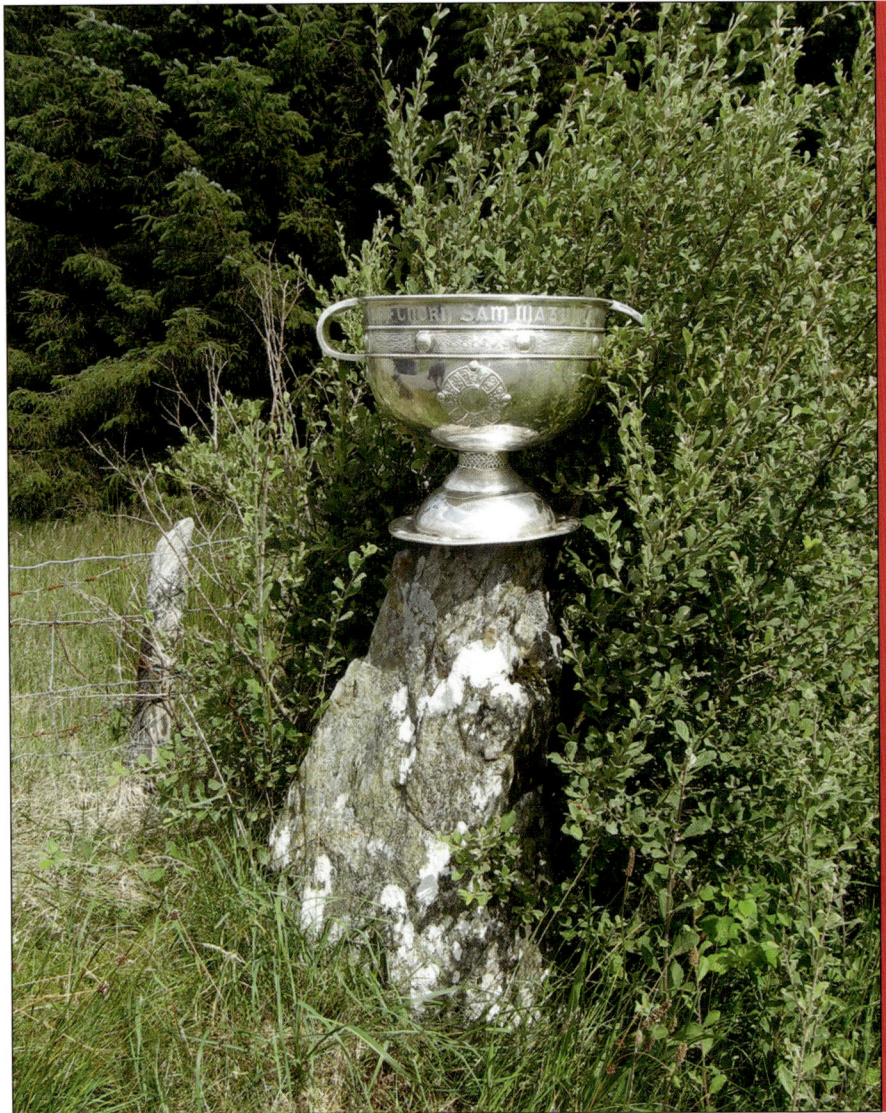

The gate creaked in the dusk. The trampled grass,
soaked and still, was disentangling
among the standing stones
after the day's excess.

Monuments were erected to mark an ancient burial site, the commemoration of an event, the marking of a ritual place, or even just a sign post.
Other standing stones close by are in Keerin and Broughderg

176

Glenmacoffer Standing Stones, Broughderg

"The two remaining stones"

The vale of Glenmacoffer

Throughout Erin's land where fair nature is so grand;
Does with beauty the green valleys cover
From fare head to cape Clare sure there's no place so dear
To me as the vale of Glenmacoffer.

Chorus
My native vale Glenmacoffer
Around you my thoughts still shall hover
Below Mullaghcharn clad with heather and fern
Lies the lovely green vale of Glenmacoffer.

(Collected by Peter Smith and Francis Clarke from the late James (Jimmy Jinny) Devlin, Fallagh, Gortin.
The vale of Glenmacoffer' was composed by Armour John Matheson, Gortin, in the early 1900's.

Cloghmore Court Tomb, (4000BC-3500BC) Carnaransy, Broughderg

Broughderg - (Bruach Derg) - Red bank

"Time honoured place"

while cattle
swayed sleepily
under low branches
lashing the ropes
of their tails
across the centuries.

Another court tomb close by is Broughderg court tomb.
The famous pipe maker who started the first workshop in Broughderg was Dan Mc Guigan (1827 – 1899).
Related to the former boxing champion Barry Mc Guigan.
Sean Clarke and Patrick Burns - Pictured.

Carnanagarranbane Double Court Tomb (4000BC - 3500BC)

Carnanagarranbane, Broughderg

"A cairn of stones in the shape of a white horse"

Ruined buildings, ruined stones,
Enclosures, tombs and natural places
In the townlands of Broughderg

Part of the tomb was used to build St Mary's chapel, Broughderg in 1885. This building is now used as a community centre.
Broughderg : Nowhere else in this island is there found such a high concentration of the stone remains of its first inhabitants;
a versatile treasure ground for the archaeologist, professional or amateur.

Keerin Portal Tomb, (Grainne's grave), (3000BC - 2500BC), Broughderg

Keerin - (caertheainn) - Boggy land on which the mountain ash grows on a moor.

A tomb is not a blind alley, it is a thoroughfare.
It closes on the twilight and opens on the dawn.

A well preserved tomb with a second tomb (Dermot's grave) nearby.

Quarry and Mini Megalithic Tomb (4000BC - 1500BC)

Broughderg - (Bruach Derg) - Red Bank

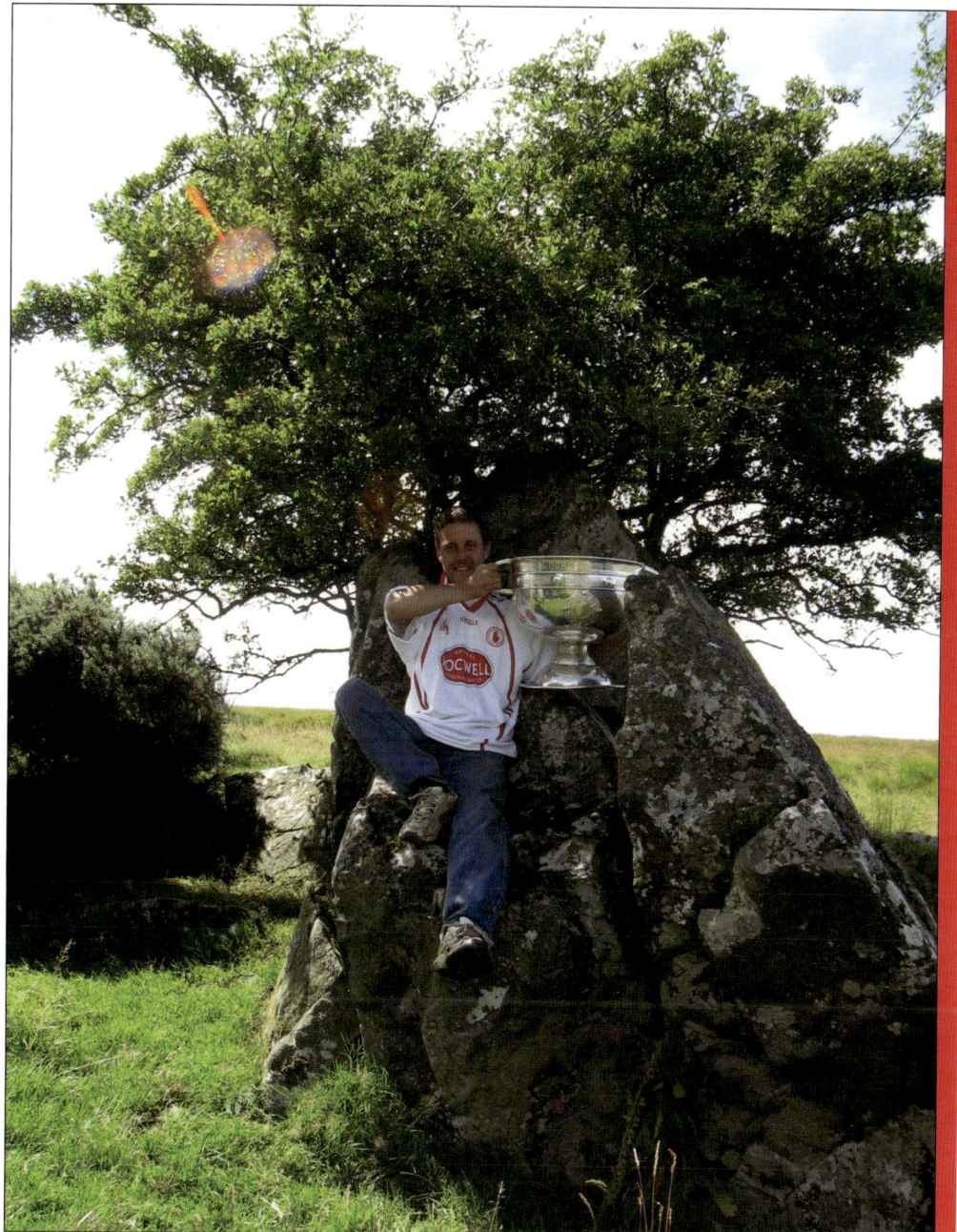

Now nature has taken back
These acreages into its keeping,
Scribbling surfaces with lichens,
Letting undergrowth spread rankly,
Restoring silence as a constant,
Apart from the birds calls.

Brendan McCullagh - Pictured

Dunmullan old church and graveyard, Omagh

Ancient ecclesiastical site dating from the 6th century

The fort of the little field

There's a place they call Dunmullan
Where my own folk used to be
There's a farm down in Dunmullan
That was paradise to me
For the Lord who set his heaven
In the clouds that hide his throne
It was he that made Dunmullan
In the county of Tyrone.

by W F Marshall
The bard of Tyrone (1888-1959)

Also known as Cappagh old Church Dunmullan
Both gables survive and on a corner there are finely carved chambered quoins or corner stones. The main body of the church dates to the 16th century but this site may have been used as a church site since the early Christian period. A bell associated with this parish, known as the Cappagh bell, is in the national museum of Ireland Dublin.

Lough Neagh

On the banks of Lough Neagh - the largest lake in these Isles

"The fishing enthusiast's paradise"

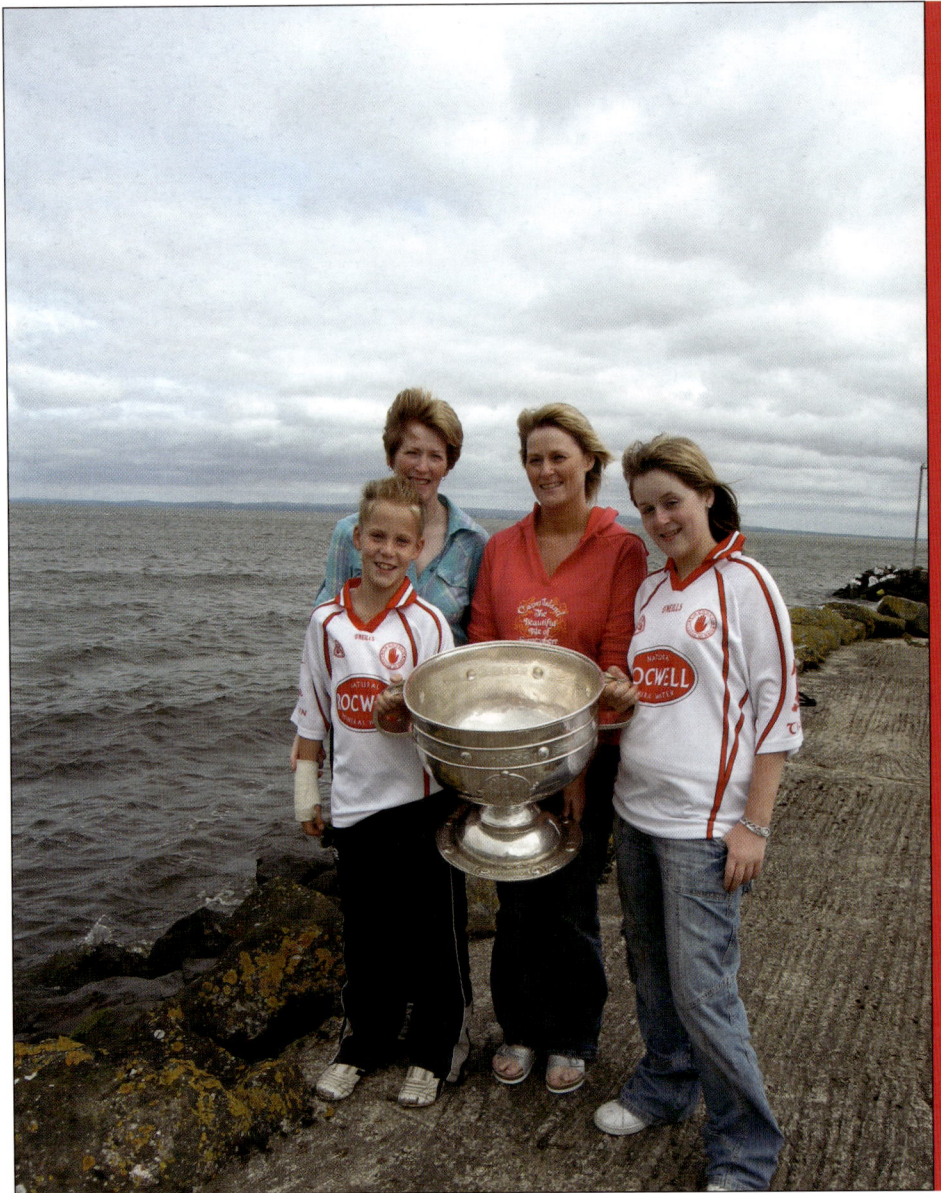

On Lough Neagh's bank, as the fisherman strays,
When the clear cold eve's declining,
He sees the round towers of other days
In the wave beneath him shining.

Exhibition and displays of the history of the Lough Neagh fishing and eel industry, can be seen at Kinturk Cultural Centre, Ballyronan.

Cregganconroe Court Tomb

Cregganconroe - (Creagancon ruaidh) - Little rock of the red hound fox

Oh the wild joys of living'
The leaping from rock to rock...
How good the child's life, the
more living how fit to employ.
All the heart
And soul and the senses
Forever in joy!

Altdrumman Portal Tomb, (Cloghogle), Loughmacrory

Cloghogle - (Cloch ogalach) - raised stone

Led to the ancient death. The capstone,
Set like a cauldron on three legs,
Was marooned by the swimming crop.
A gust and the cromlech floated,
Motionless at time's moorings.

Loughmacrory Lake, Loughmacrory

Loughmacrory - (Loch mha Ruain) - Mac Ruain's lake

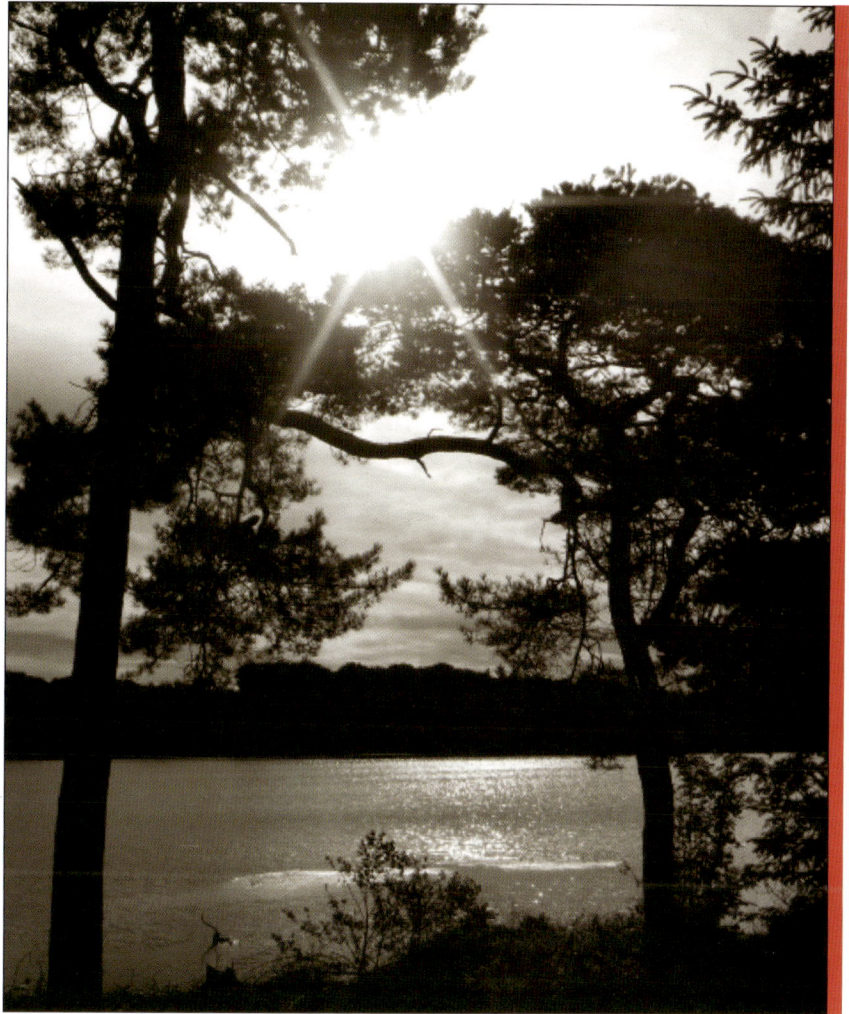

A little lonely moorland lake
Its waters brown and cool and deep-
The cliff, the hills behind it, make
A picture from my heart to keep.

by Rose Kavanagh

Three holy wells close by are known as
St Stephen's Well, St Eugene's (or St.Eoin's) Well and St Brigid's Well.

Saint Patricks Chapel, Dungannon

Designed by J.J. McCarthy (1867), in a French Gothic Style, from the 13th century.
It was completed by his son Charles J McCarthy (1889).
The church was designed to accommodate about 4000 people.

The contractor was Mr Thomas Byrne of Belfast

St. Macartan's Chapel, Augher

St Macartans Chapel was built in 1846. It was the first Catholic Cathedral in the diocese of Clogher after the catholic emancipation in 1829.

Rocwell Natural Mineral Water

Pomeroy

"Water; the source of life"

"Sure, it's only Natural"

The Quinn Family
Rocwell Mineral Water Company, Pomeroy

Cool water from the sandstone rock,
Always a steady flow,
Water as clear as crystal,
Cool as the morning dew.

by Frances Gibson

Goles Stone Row, Cranagh, Plumbridge

Cranagh - (Cranach) - A place abounding in trees

*The Standing Stones
keep well their secrets
teasing with memories
that only the dead
can know.*

Other Bronze age monuments include Carnanelly, Cranagh stone alignment, Castledamph and Aghalane stone circles and Clogherny Glebe cemetery.

Bridge over Glenelly River

There is not in the wide world ,a valley so sweet
As the vale in whose bosom the bright waters meet,
Oh! The last rays of feeling and life must depart
E're the bloom of the valley shall fade from my heart.

by Thomas Moore
Irish songwriter (1779-1852)

Paidi Laidir Mc Cullagh (1882-1958) of Curraghinalt Rouskey was the best Irish speaker in the whole of the Glenelly; a blacksmith, cooper, saddler, shoemaker and poteen maker. He was the only person in the area who could master the craftsmanship of rush and straw. He made a 'An Sugan Droma' - a horse's harness from the tail to the shoulders. It is now in the museum in Daingean Co. Offaly. He is buried in Rouskey Graveyard.

Land of Owen;
Something not made
with hands-a mountain,
the curve of the stream

She is a rich and rare land,
Oh, she's fresh and fair land;
She is a dear and rare land,
This native land of mine.

by Thomas Davis
Irish Poet (1814 - 1845)

Creggandevesky Court Tomb, Carrickmore

Creggandevesky - (Creagain dubh uisge) - Stoney place of black water

Built about 5500 years ago

Midsummer past, the days reach out
Towards the autumn glow
Of golden corn and falling leaves
That lead to winter's snow.
So let us grasp the precious hours
While the season lingers on,
And keep the sunshine in our hearts
Long after summer's gone.

Creggandevesky is one of Irelands best located and preserved court tombs, overlooking a lake and with wide views over the peaty, wilderness-like lowlands around the Sperrin mountains. There is also a nineteenth century sweat house in Creggandevesky.

*Lifelong pleasures of the countryside
and the wonders of wildlife and tombs*

Tyrone Panel: 2003 All-Ireland Final

1 John Devine
2 Cairan Gourley
3 Cormac McAnallen
4 Ryan McMenamin
5 Conor Gormley
6 Gavin Devlin
7 Phillip Jordan
8 Kevin Hughes
9 Sean Cavanagh
10 Brian Dooher
11 Brian McGuigan
12 Gerard Cavlan
13 Enda McGinley
14 Peter Canavan (Cap.)
15 Eoin Mulligan

Subs:
16 Pascal McConnell
17 Dermot Carlin
18 Mark Harte
19 Colin Holmes
20 Paul Horisk
21 Chris Lawn
22 Peter Loughran
23 Declan McCrossan
24 Michael McGee
25 Cormac McGinley
26 Frank McGuigan
27 Seamus Mulgrew
28 Stephen O'Neill
29 Brian Robinson
30 Michael Coleman

Manager: Mickey Harte
(Team as of September 2003 versus Armagh)

Tyrone Panel: 2005 All-Ireland Finall

1 Pascal McConnell
2 Ryan McMenamin
3 Joe McMahon
4 Michael McGee
5 David Harte
6 Conor Gormley
7 Phillip Jordan
8 Enda McGinley
9 Sean Cavanagh
10 Brian Dooher (Cap.)
11 Brian McGuigan
12 Ryan Mellon
13 Peter Canavan
14 Stephen O'Neill
15 Eoin Mulligan

Subs:
16 John Devine
17 Eoghain Bradley
18 Brian Meenan
19 Gavin Devlin
20 Brendan Donnelly
21 Peter Donnelly
22 Cairan Gourley
23 Mark Harte
24 Colin Holmes
25 Chris Lawn
26 Colm McCullagh
27 Leo Meenan
28 Michael Murphy
29 Martin Penrose
30 Shane Sweeney

Manager: Mickey Harte
(Team as of September 2005 versus Kerry)

We are deeply appreciative of all people who were willingly photographed with the Sam Maguire cup.
Many also assisted with their advice and written information on topics/areas of interest in Co Tyrone.
Our thanks to them all.

Selected poems reproduced by the kind
permission of the Kearney family

Photography

Frank Quinn
Kathleen Burns
Aiden Molloy

Additional Photography by

Ken Williams
Jim Dunne
Chris Curran
Tyrone Crystal, Killybrackey, Dungannon - www.tyronecrystal.com
Killymaddy Tourist Information Centre
Omagh Tourist Centre
Strabane Tourist Centre
Sperrin Tourism, Burnavon, Cookstown
Sperrin Tourism, Moneymore - www.sperrinstourism.com

This is the journey, now is the time
New paths to follow and mountains to climb
Travelling onwards enjoying each mile
Rejoicing in the moment the journey was worthwhile.

We dedicate this book to the
Tyrone Senior All Ireland Football Champions of 2003 and 2005
The manager Micky Harte and his management team
Tyrone County Chairman, Pat Darcy
Former Tyrone Chairman, Dominic Mc Caughey
Club Tyrone, Tyrone County Board and the wider G.A.A fraternity in Tyrone

We would like to take this opportunity to congratulate
Omagh Christain Brothers School in winning the 2007 Hogan cup
and the Tyrone Vocational Schools in winning the All Ireland in 2007

Acknowledgements

The assistance of the following who did research work,
supplied materials, or photographs or otherwise helped in
the production of the book is gratefully appreciated.

Dr Seamus O'Caithain
Pat Darcy
Dr Peter J Smith
Mr Francis Clarke
Mr &Mrs Patsy O'Rourke, Brefni house, Killyman
Mr Terry Mc Shane, Killyman
Sister Marian O'Hagan, Convent of Mercy, Dungannon
Mr Kieran Lynch, Shantamey, Ballygawley
Ms Oonagh Mc Nally, Tyrone Crystal, Dungannon
Chris Curran, All-Star Publications Ltd., Omagh,
Flavour of Tyrone Ltd, Killymaddy Tourist Information Centre, Ballygawley Road, Dungannon
Sperrin Tourism, Burnavon, Cookstown
Strabane Tourism Centre, Strabane
Sperrin Tourism Centre, Moneymore
Omagh Tourism Centre, Omagh
Sperrin Heritage Centre, Cranagh

Libraries
Dungannon local library, Cookstown Library, Omagh County library
Cardinal Tomas O'Fiach library, Armagh
Irish History Library, Abbey Street, Armagh

We are grateful to those who have given advise or
took the time to locate historical places of Tyrone

Mr Sean Clarke, Greencastle
Mr John Donaghy, An Creagan Centre
Mr Paddy Grugan, Carrickmore
Mr Charlie Donnelly, Galbally

We are happy to acknowledge people whom we met along the way
and gave their time for discussion on various areas in Tyrone.

Seamus and Teresa Anderson, Moymore
Brian and Pamela Clarke, Aghafad
Joseph Clarke, Aghafad
Austin and Michelle O'Kane, Murnells
Louis Conway, Tulnacross Road, Dunamore
Mr Donal Monaghan, Tulnacross Road, Dunamore

Felix Hagan and his family circle for his contribution and information about
the mass garden in Munderadoe.

Collected poems (1995)
by kind permission of the author, Mr John Montague and The Gallery Press,
Loughcrew, Oldcastle, County Meath.

To our brother Michael Quinn for his inspirational advice.

Bibliography

Environment And Heritage Service DOE, N. Ireland

Broughderg a place and its peoples : Sean Clarke

Bi-centenary of St. Brigid's Church Killyman (1786-1986)

Souvenir booklet of the mass in Munderdoe Mass Garden, Pomeroy : Edited by Felix Hagan

Guide to National and Historic monuments of Ireland : Peter Harbison

An Tearmann IV Parish magazine of Termonmaguirk : Editor P. O Grugan

St. Colmcille 597-1997: An Tearmann, Parish of Termonmaguirk.

The Laragh Burn, Poems, Pictures and Stories from Mid-Tyrone : By Mick Grimes

Celtic Sacred Landscape By Nigel Pennick

The Traveller's Guide to Sacred Ireland Cary Meehan

Irish place names : Deidre & Laurence Flanagan

The heart of Tyrone by Tullyneil : Irish Studies Library, Armagh

Understanding Historical monuments on the farm

Townland names of County Tyrone

Selected Poems by James Clarence Mangan

More poems from the Irish by The Earl of Longford

A selection of poems by Felix Kearney

Collected Poems by John Montague

Rose Kavanagh and her verses.

Reflections on Irelands Heritage by Frances Gibson

Voices from the hedgegrows : A book of verse by Tyrone Poets

Poems from W.F. Marshall

Poems from William Carleton

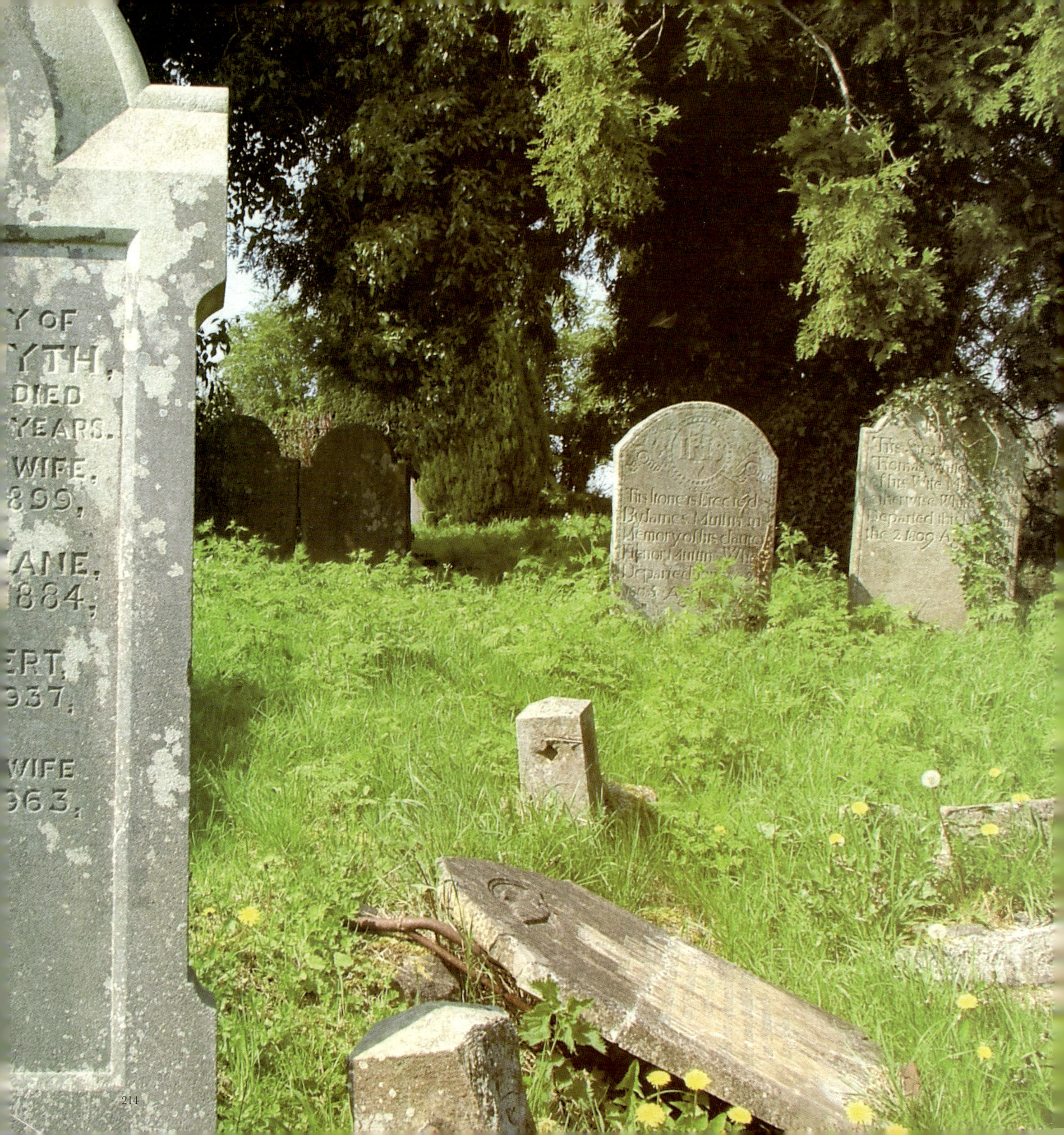
Y OF
YTH,
DIED
YEARS.
WIFE,
899,
ANE,
1884,
ERT,
937,
WIFE
963,

Now they are gone, those mighty men,
Those people of all they saw,
And only we are left to walk
This high and winding lonely lane,
Whilst all around, on deep-etched hills
Their proud, immortal marks remain